Restoring the Woven Cord

Strands of Celtic Christianity
for the Church today

Text copyright © Michael Mitton 1995, 2010
Illustrations copyright © Lindsey Attwood 1995
The author asserts the moral right
to be identified as the author of this work

Published by
The Bible Reading Fellowship
15 The Chambers, Vineyard
Abingdon OX14 3FE
United Kingdom
Tel: +44 (0)1865 319700
Fax: +44 (0)1865 319701
Email: enquiries@brf.org.uk
Website: www.brf.org.uk

ISBN 978 1 84101 800 3
First published 1995 by Darton, Longman and Todd
Revised edition published 2010
Reprinted 2013
10 9 8 7 6 5 4 3 2 1

Acknowledgments
Unless otherwise stated, scripture quotations are taken from The Holy Bible, New
International Version copyright © 1973, 1978, 1984 by International Bible Society, and used
by permission of Hodder & Stoughton Publishers, a member of the Hachette Livre UK Group.
All rights reserved. 'NIV' is a registered trademark of International Bible Society. UK trademark
number 1448790.

Scripture quotations from The New Revised Standard Version of the Bible, Anglicised Edition,
copyright © 1989, 1995 by the Division of Christian Education of the National Council of
the Churches of Christ in the United States of America, are used by permission. All rights
reserved.

A catalogue record for this book is available from the British Library

Printed by Lightning Source

Restoring the
Woven Cord

Strands of Celtic Christianity
for the Church today

Michael Mitton

For John Peet: You inspired me so much when I was writing this book.
You are now in Paradise, but you continue to inspire me
and I remember you with affection and gratitude.

Acknowledgments

Thanks are due to The Community of Aidan and Hilda for permission to use prayers from various liturgies. Further details of The Community of Aidan and Hilda can be found at www.aidanandhilda.org.uk

Thanks are also due to Lindsey Attwood for her illustrations. She has combined a remarkable talent with a deep appreciation of the Celtic way and a lovely openness to the Holy Spirit who has so clearly inspired her. For further details of Lindsey's work, go to www.lindseyattwood.co.uk.

Preface to the Second Edition

It is 15 years since this book was first published. I wrote it while I was Director of Anglican Renewal Ministries, and I was interested in exploring models of renewal that would be relevant for the late 20th-century Anglican Church. I found in the stories of the Celtic saints a rich heritage, which gave inspiration for how the church could be renewed in the emerging post-Christendom era. While I was personally convinced that God was directing our attention to this heritage, I was not sure how many others would share the conviction. Would the themes I was writing about resonate with my readers, or would they politely put the book to one side and assume I was suffering from a midlife crisis that was expressing itself in a bout of nostalgia?

As it turned out, I was utterly amazed by the response. I have written a number of books but this one evoked more response than any of the others. I had letters from Protestants and Catholics, traditionalists and charismatics, people from brand new churches and those from established old churches, all telling me that God had spoken powerfully to them through the stories of the saints described in the book. People from both liberal and evangelical traditions also wrote to me, often using expressions like 'I feel I have come home'.

During that time, I was asked to speak at a number of meetings, conferences and retreats. I started to get anxious that people would view me as a 'Celtic expert', despite my assurances that I was an explorer, not an expert. I also saw the danger that Celtic Christianity could too easily become esoteric and cultic, attracting people who wore Celtic crosses and jewellery, used only Celtic prayers and would compete in their knowledge of Celtic saints. It would all be a long way from the simplicity of Aidan, who, after all, wasn't trying to promote Celtic Christianity; he was simply following the Jesus of the Beatitudes. I sensed God calling me to stop my studies of Celtic Christianity and simply use the vision I had received to integrate it into my Christian life. I could see that God was calling other people to engage in different ways with all of this. For example, my good friend Ray Simpson, who writes in this new edition of the book, was undoubtedly called to be a researcher and pioneer about the Celtic way, and he has worked tirelessly at helping us to integrate the Celtic way practically into our 21st-century church life.

In time, I was called from my work with Anglican Renewal Ministries to the Acorn Christian Healing Foundation, where God led me into a deeper experience of the ministry of healing that included a six-year training experience in the value of listening as I headed up Acorn's Christian Listeners. Throughout this time, the Celtic fire at the heart of my spiritual life has never diminished. As I work on this revised edition of the book, I have now launched out in a coracle of freelance ministry, and once again I have found that I have needed to go back to my brothers and sisters of faith who roamed these lands so many years ago, yet whose inspiring influence on my life is as alive as ever. This new work includes the responsibility of encouraging and supporting Fresh Expressions of church life in the diocese of Derby. I am also leading a small local church that was, not long ago, struggling for breath, but now, by the grace of God, is returning to life. Both my local and wider church roles have deepened my conviction that the themes outlined in this book are essential if the church is to become the mission community that it so desperately needs to be.

I also note with great interest how God has been building on this Celtic vision over the last 15 years, and how every denomination and church stream has been affected. Iona and Lindisfarne continue to draw large numbers of visitors and pilgrims; Celtic liturgies appear regularly in church worship; communities such as the Northumbria Community and the Community of Aidan and Hilda are flourishing. There is no sense that we were going through a short-lived Celtic phase or fashion in the mid-1990s. Something much more long-lasting is happening. My hope is that, in time, 'Celtic Christianity' as a distinct spirituality will die in the church and instead become so integrated that we won't think of it as 'different' as it permeates the life of the church at different levels. I am now convinced that the popularising of Celtic spirituality that began at the end of the last century is a vital part of God's transforming his church to become what it was always meant to be.

There have, of course, been concerns about the growth of interest in Celtic Christian spirituality, not least from those who know a lot about the subject. Philip Sheldrake wrote his *Living Between the Worlds* in the same year that I wrote my book and he warns, 'There is a danger that either we force the history and tradition of particular spiritualities into the shape of other, modern experiences or we seek to shape our own contemporary spiritual quest naively in terms of some presumed golden age.'[1]

Similarly, Ian Bradley, in his *Celtic Christianity—Making Myths and Chasing Dreams*, writes, 'Romantic nostalgia and wishful thinking remain key elements in the contemporary revival [of Celtic Christianity], with new concerns such as feminism and ecological awareness being projected on to the Celtic Church alongside more long-lasting themes like primitive simplicity, closeness to nature and openness to other religious traditions.'[2]

He goes on to mention the less edifying side 'in the commercialism that has packaged and marketed Celtic Christianity as a commodity to sell books, compact discs and religious trinkets to promote the burgeoning heritage and tourist industries'.[3] He notes that, perhaps in reaction to this, we have seen a sharper divergence between popular and academic treatments of the subject, and in recent years I have listened to academic lectures that question even if there was such a thing as a Celtic Church.

These concerns must be carefully considered but none of them has caused me to change what I wrote in 1995. Even then, I was very anxious about the likely romanticisation and commercialisation of this spiritual tradition, and to some extent I confess that in my enthusiasm I might have contributed to both perils. We do need to be rigorous and honest in our reading of these old stories and do all we can to avoid harnessing them for our own particular enthusiasms. But as the years go by, for me, these stories still stand bold and strong, having their effect on my life and on the lives of countless others, and in the main this effect is drawing people closer to God. It is helping people to find a natural place of belonging and it is inspiring us to reach out in styles of mission that are sensitive, compassionate and powerful. What continues to be vital, I find, is the holding together of the different strands, and we would do a great disservice to this tradition if we simply enthused about one strand and ignored the others.

So why republish this book? It is because of the response I have witnessed in people over the past 15 years. It is because of what I see God doing in people's lives as they catch a vision of a gentle Aidan-like Christianity that is full of the grace of God. It is because I believe that we desperately need authentic expressions of our faith in a society that has so painfully lost its way. It is because I believe, more than ever, that the expression of faith that God gave this nation when he first breathed his Spirit across the land is the best template we can find for a people who have turned their backs on the institutional church, yet have a vulnerable openness to the possibility of a God of love being involved in their lives. In short, millions of people need to meet the Jesus of the Gospels—not the Jesus of the cold traditionalism that has forced so many humble-hearted people away from God; not the Jesus of the 'thou shalt not', unkind judgmentalism that has caused too many to distrust the church and keep well clear of it; not the Jesus of hyped-up renewal that makes promises that can't be kept and leaves people with bitter disappointments. The Jesus of the Gospels was well introduced to us by the likes of Aidan, Hilda, Columba and Brigid, and I happen to think that they are among the best guides for us in this postmodern culture. They weren't perfect and, like all of us, had normal human weaknesses. Among their qualities that speak to us today, they demonstrated a good and careful listening, both to the leading of the Spirit of God and, compassionately, to the people of the land. As a result, they developed an expression of church that made sense to the people and showed them clearly that there is a God in heaven who has noticed them, so much so that he has chosen to live among them to understand the nitty-gritty of everyday life, who has died for them, and who empowers them with the kind of love that transforms their lives here on earth and gives a hope for eternity. Because they were such clear exponents of this gospel message through their words and deeds, we do well to listen to them today.

In revising this book, I have decided to reorder the chapters so that the stories progress chronologically (more or less, as some dates are not clear). I'm grateful to David Adam, who, in a press review, pointed out a couple of inaccuracies in the original book, and I have amended these. I fear that there will still be some lurking within these covers, but I have done my best to get the facts right.

I am most grateful to four friends who have contributed to an extended afterword to this reprint. I have chosen authors from different fields of life and service and I provide a brief introduction to each one at the start of their piece. Two are from the UK and two from overseas, to demonstrate the international nature of the interest in Celtic Christianity. I am grateful to all of them for their very thoughtful input into this book.

On a recent visit to Lindisfarne, I walked the two-and-a-half-mile journey from the mainland to the island, following the straight line of the waymarks. As I did so, I thought much about Aidan journeying over the sand and clay, no doubt praying for the gospel to be spread far and wide from this small outpost, and I found myself in wonder at the extraordinary effectiveness of that time of mission. At the end of the walk, I wrote these lines, which might set the mood as we set out to explore the Celtic way through the stories in this book:

And it was hope
that led him to take yet more steps
in the slippery clay.
The north-east breeze
summoned up prophecy
from centuries before him
about centuries after him.
He, caught in the middle
between mainland and island,
knew he had come as priest;
kneeling he wept
with the seagulls and seals
till the turning tide bade him on.

Later, the salt water concealed his footprints
while he, safe on his island,
gripped his staff and raised his burning torch
and for a time
the whole land was ablaze
while estuary angels flooded inland
and the seas of blessing
left their rich sediment.

For a time the earth knew it was loved
and breathed well.

Contents

⊕

— 1 —

The strands of our faith

In March 1992, I set off on a journey that changed the direction of my life. I travelled to the holy island of Lindisfarne, which lies just south of the Scottish border, not far from my birthplace, Edinburgh. Here, during the course of two blustery wet and cold days, I became acquainted with this historic place, researching the lives of Aidan and Cuthbert who had lived here during the Christian dawn of the isles of Britain and Ireland. For me it was like a homecoming. Something about the island and its history connected with a deep longing within me and brought together many different strands of my own faith.

As I explored the Celtic faith of this ancient mission centre, I discovered something that I had been searching for during the past 20 years. I had been searching for an expression of faith in which I could own the various strands that have become so important for me. I discovered a burning and evangelical love for the Bible; I discovered a depth of spiritual life and stillness that I had encountered in Catholic and Anglo-Catholic spirituality; I discovered a radical commitment to the poor and to God's creation, and I discovered the most attractive expression of charismatic life that I had yet encountered. Not only this, but I felt connected with my roots for the first time. As a Protestant I had never felt entirely comfortable with finding my spiritual roots in the religious and political protests of the 16th century, particularly as I am good friends with a number of Roman Catholics and have a great respect for their church. I have always felt awkwardness about our history and a pain at our separation. Yet here, in the Celtic church, there are common roots that go back long before our days of separation.

But was this feeling just personal to me? Was my interest in Celtic Christianity just an odd quirk, an indication of midlife crisis? During the course of the ensuing two years, I started to speak publicly about Celtic Christianity and was reassured to discover a widespread and growing interest in the subject. I am now convinced that all this is much more than just an odd quirk. I am in no doubt that the Spirit of God is reminding us of the first expression of faith in these isles to give us inspiration for Christian ministry and mission today. While it had its faults, I believe that the early Celtic church was the nearest thing in our Christian history to a complete expression of faith in this country. After all, no other church has had such impact on this land, steadily converting the country from Druid-led paganism to Christianity. Extraordinarily, many of us have been brought up on the notion of the 'Dark Ages', with an implication that little of spiritual worth happened in this land until the Reformation. Nothing could be further from the truth. For Britain, the period from the fifth to the ninth centuries should be seen as the 'Light Ages' in which, arguably, a light shone that was brighter than any since.

There is, of course, a real danger of romanticising the Celtic church and overlooking its weaknesses. Also, we should not generalise too much as there were variations within it. For example, there were differences between the Lindisfarne-based mission that began with Aidan and the Iona-based mission that started with Columba, and personally I am more attracted to the Lindisfarne mission.

Christian beginnings in Britain

Some of the Roman legions stationed in Britain were Christians and we have evidence of a Christian presence in this land from the earliest times. In Manchester Museum, there is a pottery shard from a Spanish amphora, inscribed with an acrostic of the Lord's Prayer in Latin, which is dated at around AD180. The second-century writer Origen refers to Christians in Britain, and at the Council of Arles in AD314 we even have mention of three British bishops. There is also the Glastonbury legend, which asserts that Joseph of Arimathea visited Britain. The legend claims that Joseph was a tin trader and made regular trips to the West Country of Britain to purchase tin. He knew Jesus as a child and brought him on one occasion to Cornwall, thus inspiring William Blake to wonder if 'those feet in ancient time' walked 'upon England's mountains green'. The story goes that, following the death and resurrection of Jesus, Joseph travelled to England again, this time carrying the Holy Grail that contained the blood and sweat of Christ, arriving eventually at the Isle of Avalon, Glastonbury. While this story is usually viewed as a quaint legend, it is not entirely implausible to believe that Joseph was a tin trader, and, as such, he is quite likely to have made journeys to the tin-rich island of Britain. Gildas, a sixth-century historian, speaks of Britain receiving the 'beams of light' of the gospel during the reign of Tiberias. Since Tiberias died in AD37, this speaks of a very early mission indeed. We shall probably never know the truth of all this, but there certainly are hints in our history that the gospel arrived in Britain and Ireland during the period of the Acts of the Apostles.

The Christianity that came with the Roman legions seems to have had little effect on the local population, who preferred their indigenous pagan ways to the religion of the conquering forces. When the Romans abandoned Britain in the early fifth century, they took the Christian faith with them. However, there were embers of faith that were ready to flame up in a remarkable way. The first flames of the early Celtic church appeared in the areas that the Romans had failed to occupy, in particular in Ireland, which they never conquered. For a time, this indigenous expression of Christian life was the only one to exist in Britain and Ireland, until the church in Western Europe, based in Rome, developed an interest in Britain. This interest stemmed partly from concern for the unevangelised tribes of Angles and Saxons pouring into Britain, and partly from unease that the British Celtic church was becoming wayward, not least in its custom of selecting a different date for Easter from the Western church. Thus Pope Gregory in Rome commissioned Bishop Augustine for his famous mission to the English. Augustine and his 40 missionary monks arrived in the south of England in AD597 and set up base at Canterbury. As we shall see from time to time in the pages of this book, the relationship between the British and Roman churches was not easy. Both churches had strengths and weaknesses and both were genuinely concerned to bring the light of Christ to these lands. There was room for both but, in time, the Roman church felt that there could be only one church, united in celebrating Easter on a common date in line with the rest of Western Europe, and it therefore sought to absorb the British church into this wider network.

By the end of the sixth century, the Roman church was flourishing in a collapsing but generally Christian empire. It seems that, soon after the conversion of the Roman Emperor Constantine in the fourth century, the Christian church started to become extraordinarily worldly, in stark contrast to the very vibrant and charismatic faith that had seen it through the terrible years of persecution under the Emperors Diocletian and Galerius. Once it had become part of the establishment, it was inclined to espouse the values of the earthly kingdom rather than the kingdom of God.

By contrast, in the East, thousands were reacting strongly against this worldliness and nominalism; they moved to the deserts, where, led by such people as Anthony and Pachomius, they set up monasteries that became oases of spiritual life and wisdom. These were the first expressions of monastic life in the Christian church. These Christians were attracted to the wilderness because of the many biblical examples of the desert journey, in particular that of Jesus after his baptism in the Jordan. The culmination of his 40-day ascetic experience was a fierce contest with the devil. The desert monks and nuns felt similarly called to these hostile wastelands, which were graphic illustrations of the spiritual wasteland of nominalism and worldliness in the church. Here on behalf of the church they did battle with Satan, pleading with God through prayer, fasting and holiness to have mercy on the church, restoring it for mission to a needy world. Both the communities and the thousands of individual hermits played a key role in the spiritual survival of the church, for not only did they act as spiritual warriors but their lives also formed models of commitment, depth and transparent holiness.

Martin, Bishop of Tours (AD371), was the first Westerner to become influenced by the Eastern monks, and founded a monastery called Marmoutier—literally meaning 'the place of the big family'. It was here that Ninian was profoundly influenced and the story of the Celtic church in Britain gets under way. With Ninian and Columba in Scotland, David, Samson and Illtyd in Wales, Patrick and Brigid in Ireland, and Aidan, Cuthbert and Hilda in England (to name only a few), the Celtic fire began to grow into a blaze with monastic groups springing up everywhere.

By the time the Roman mission arrived in Canterbury, the Celtic church was looking to the East rather than the West for its inspiration. In fact, for a time, the Roman mission was effective only in the south: the centre, the north and the rest of Britain and Ireland were unreachable owing to the ravages of Anglo-Saxon invasions and frequent outbreaks of plague. It was only with the settling of the Saxons that the Roman church began to see the possibility of establishing one church in Britain, celebrating one Easter. The Roman church eventually persuaded the Celtic leaders to gather for a synod where it could all be thrashed out. Thus, in 664 both sides met at Whitby. There the increasingly powerful Wilfrid, who was forming dioceses and monasteries based on Roman models, was far more competent at arguing his case than the typically humble Celtic leaders. In many respects it was at this council that the spiritual fate of our land was decided. The Celtic church lost against the powers of Rome. The community-based church committed to poverty could not stand against the hierarchical and centrally organised church that had such effective links with secular power. But the Celtic fire still burned for many years after Whitby. In fact, it has remained alight in the 'Celtic fringes' through the ages and is now showing every sign of being rekindled across the land, and indeed across the world today.

The conflict in the early Christian era in Britain and Ireland was between Celt and Roman. Let's be absolutely clear that, when we talk of the Roman church, we are not referring to the modern-day Roman Catholic Church. We are talking about a church of 1000 years before the Reformation. The Roman church of the Middle Ages has influenced most of the Western church, Catholic *and* Protestant. In this book we are interested in how the indigenous church of Britain and Ireland expressed its faith before it become absorbed into the wider Rome-based church, and we shall see that in many ways we can still discern in the life and witness of our church today, in every denomination and church stream, characteristics of the Roman church that are now being challenged by the growth of Celtic Christianity.

Strands of faith

The Celts were great lovers of art and they loved intricate patterns. Such artwork can be found in the Book of Kells and the Lindisfarne Gospels, whose illuminations are based on wonderful and intricate strands that are interwoven to form the most beautiful patterns, full of vitality and meaning. We see the same in other expressions of Celtic Christian art that have survived to this day, such as the engraved high crosses found in Ireland and parts of Britain, which were covered with interwoven designs.

These patterns clearly depict the Celts' love of wholeness and say something very important to the church today about how these people lived their Christian lives. They had discovered the many different strands of our faith and woven them together in a most effective cord for ministry and mission. A strong cord needs many strands, but the weakness of the church through the ages is that it has tended to focus on only one or two strands at the cost of losing others. Since the collapse of the Celtic church, it seems that one generation after another made the discovery of a lost strand and, holding it up, said, 'This is the main cord'; then, rather than weaving it in to the whole, each generation dropped the others and made a rope out of only one strand, which of course will never have sufficient strength. Thus, for example, we have evangelical discoveries of justification by faith at the Reformation; we have catholic discoveries about worship and sacraments in the 19th-century Oxford Movement; we have liberal discoveries about social justice and radical witness to the poor in the 20th century; we have pentecostal/charismatic discoveries also in the last hundred years. All these have been good and necessary discoveries, but usually each group has discovered only one or two strands of the whole cord, and has forged its identity by denouncing the other strands, thus rendering the cord weak again. In the Celtic church we find a community of faith that was refreshingly free of prejudice and open to welcoming many strands into the cord of faith.

We need to study the early Celtic church in the spirit of its Christian life—with total openness to the wind of the Spirit, who may well draw our attention to strands of our Christian faith that we have too easily ignored or discarded. It is no use, for example, delighting in the love for creation without taking due note of the early church's understanding of dark powers that could despoil creation. Similarly, it would be wrong to delight in the miraculous stories of healing without studying the believers' commitment to community, the context for the healing ministry. We will need to explore with a great sense of openness.

My hope is that this book will help us discover some very important strands of our faith that were so clearly evident in the Celtic church. Of equal importance is the weaving of the strands together in our personal walk with God and in the life of the church. I have not identified all the strands, but I have chosen 14 that I happen to think are important for us to consider at this time. They are in chronological order of the saints associated with them, which I hope makes clear that there is no preference for one strand over another. Each chapter is simply a snapshot of the early Celtic church, to give some idea of how that church experienced this particular strand of Christian faith.

In this book, when I refer to the 'Celtic church' I normally mean the Celtic church that existed in Britain and Ireland roughly from the fifth to the ninth centuries AD. I am aware that, for many Christians today who live in Cornwall, Wales, Ireland and Scotland, the Celtic church is not in the past but is alive and well in the present. Although there are some references to the modern Celtic church, I am mainly concerning myself with the early church in this book.

I have called the book *Restoring the Woven Cord* because it is my deep conviction that the Celtic church challenges us to rediscover the strands of our faith and find ways of weaving them together in our personal lives and the life of our churches. Those who know much more than I do about weaving and rope work will tell me that you cannot technically weave a cord. Well, I know, but I think of it more poetically than literally! We need the strong cord with its many strands; we need the interweaving to take place in our own lives.

Each chapter has four ingredients, as follows.

Story and reflection

Story was most important to the Celtic church. They taught by means of stories, songs, poems and pictures. Pre-Christian Celts had very little interest in writing, which is one reason why it is difficult to research their history. But their oral tradition was strong and they delighted in storytelling, which they viewed as an imaginative way of communicating truth. Each chapter of this book therefore has one leading story from the Celtic church, and I will use this, along with various other stories, to discuss the theme of the chapter. You will find that my main resource is the Venerable Bede, which reflects my admiration for him. My special interest is in the early Celtic church in Northumbria and this is why I regularly return to stories from this church. Also, because Bede wrote such a thorough account of Cuthbert's life, this particular saint features more regularly than others. I am sorry that only two female saints appear in the main stories. This is simply because most of the stories we have are about male saints, but, as we shall see in Chapter 11, this does not at all reflect the Celtic church's estimation of women, which was very high. The story in each chapter provides a basis for the theme that I explore in the pages following, where my aim is to connect the understanding and experience of that particular theme in the early Celtic church with our world today.

Bible reading

There is a Bible reading that connects with the theme of each chapter. This can be used as guidance for the application section.

Application

This section contains three questions that will help to apply the theme of the chapter to your situation. You can use these questions for your own reflection or as starter questions if you are using the book for group study.

Prayer

All the prayers are kindly provided by The Community of Aidan and Hilda, written either by Ray Simpson or myself (apart from Columba's in Chapter 7). I hope that each prayer will lead into further prayers as you take the themes of the strand and weave it into your own life and witness.

Drawing

Each chapter includes a drawing by Lindsey Attwood. Lindsey has produced these drawings after prayerfully considering each theme. You can use them for your own prayer and meditation, following the Celtic way of hearing God through picture as well as word.

⊕

Prayer

Patrick

There is some speculation about the dates of Patrick's life and ministry, and such is the weave of historical fact and legendary tale about the life of this great missionary that it is hard to discern firm details of his life. However, there is a consensus that he was clearly a very great evangelist and pastor, and he is one of the few early Celtic Christians who have left us a written record of their own life and ministry.

It is generally believed that Patrick was a British Celt, born sometime around the turn of the fourth and fifth centuries in the north-west of Britain. It was common in those days for people to go to other lands and grab a few healthy young lads to take home as slaves. Thus it was that a group of Irish slave traders captured Patrick when he was 16 and he came into the possession of a chieftain named Milch. He was put to work herding cattle in County Antrim, and here, rather like the prodigal son, he 'returned with a whole heart to the Lord my God'. It was here on the slopes of Slemish, near Ballymena, that Patrick experienced an extraordinary surge of prayer, as he records in his *Confession*:

But after I had come to Ireland I daily used to feed cattle, and I prayed frequently during the day; the love of God and the fear of Him increased more and more, and faith became stronger, and the spirit was stirred; so that one day I said about a hundred prayers, and in the night nearly the same; so that I used even to remain in the woods and in the mountains;

before daylight I used to rise to prayer, through snow, through frost, through rain, and I felt no harm; nor was there any slothfulness in me, as I now perceive, because the spirit was then fervent within me.[1]

Patrick tells us that one night, during this intense period of prayer, he had a dream that he would return home. He duly escaped and caught a boat to France, where he trained as a priest. He then returned to Britain, when he had a further prophetic dream. In this dream he saw a man coming from Ireland who gave a letter to Patrick entitled 'The Voice of the Irish'. As he read the letter, he heard the voice of many Irish people beckoning him to come and walk among them. This dream was his call to Ireland and, following his consecration as bishop, he arrived in AD435, probably at Strangford Lough. Throughout the next three decades he engaged in the most vigorous and effective evangelistic work and, when he died in 461, he left behind him thousands of baptised Christians and many communities that were blossoming into life.

The prayer life of the early Celtic church is worthy of the admiration of Christians of every tradition. In this church we find hermits leading austere lives of fasting and contemplative prayer. We also find Pentecostal-style enthusiastic prayer. Perhaps the Celtic church, more than any other, was true to Paul's exhortation to the Ephesians to 'pray in the Spirit on all occasions with all kinds of prayers and requests' (Ephesians 6:18, NIV).

The hermit and ascetic life

Possibly the clearest witness to the vital role of prayer was in the life and ministry of the hermit. It is no surprise that a church so closely connected with the Desert Fathers should see such a flourishing of eremetical life. St Anthony, the first and most renowned Desert Father, who lived to be over 100 years old despite his austere life in the Egyptian desert, was greatly loved and admired by the Celtic church. The ancient high crosses of Monasterboice in Ireland are carved with the images of two saints—Anthony and Paul of Thebes, both Desert Fathers. The Celtic church found such people a great inspiration and, although the climate of northern Europe was very different from the hot deserts of Egypt, the principles of desert spirituality could be applied. Martin Palmer writes:

In many parts of Ireland, Wales and Scotland you can find tiny chapels of the remains of hermitages in the most remote and desolate places. Quite often these places will bear names such as Dysart, Disserth or the like. These words are all corruptions of the word desert. And they were so called because in the Celtic monastic tradition, to go to a remote place for spiritual retreat was to go into the desert. The idea of going to the desert is a direct link back to the Coptic monks. [2]

Some would seek these deserts for short periods of time. For example, it seems to have been the custom of Celtic bishops to go to a 'desert' during Lent in fasting and prayer. Thus Cuthbert and his successor on Lindisfarne, Eadbert, would go to the island now called 'Cuddy's Isle', a little tidal island a few metres from Lindisfarne. Here they, and many after them, would spend short or longer periods of time in prayer and quietness. For Cuthbert, it was the precursor to a more prolonged solitary life, as he eventually felt called to go to an island further out to sea, Farne Island, which Aidan had used as a place of retreat. Cuthbert lived on this island for almost ten years before he was persuaded to return to the mainland and become a bishop. Bede tells us that Cuthbert went to Farne Island for 'solitary contemplation and silence'. He was not alone all the time; it seems that he had regular visits from the Lindisfarne community. Members of the community would go over to help him build his dwelling and his chapel, and to prepare the land so that he could grow his own food. It seems that Cuthbert actually became more and more remote on Farne Island, eventually building a high-walled, open-roofed dwelling for himself, and even blocking up the window so that when monks came to visit him he could not see their faces. All he saw was the sky, as he kept his gaze towards heaven.

Such asceticism was common in the Celtic church, though we do not have many records of some of the most bizarre forms of ascetic behaviour that took place in the East. The ascetic life, lived out in some remote and, frankly, fairly hostile places encouraged a sense of doing battle in the wilderness, following the example of the Lord, but the close proximity to the forces of nature also had the effect of quickening the spirit in prayer. Patrick's early experience of praying in the bleakness of winter is an example of this. His contact with the cold frosts made him more sharply aware of the cold hearts of his captors and, by contrast, the compassionate and warm heart of God. Cuthbert's hours spent praying in the cold sea may seem absurd to those who are accustomed to saying their prayers in the comfort of a fireside armchair, but there is no doubt that the experience fuelled a fire within him which quite probably literally warmed him up.

This kind of asceticism is a form of fasting. Not everyone in the Celtic communities lived ascetic lives but all would regularly fast. Asceticism widened the arena of fasting to include celibacy and the withdrawal of human comforts. Fasting has the effect of making the spirit more alert to God, and there is no doubt that Cuthbert and others were spiritually highly sensitive.

When he eventually left Farne Island, Cuthbert's place was taken by Ethelwald. Such places were sanctified by holy people and they became like spiritual watchtowers. If one hermit left, another would come and take his or her place, standing guard in prayer.

In our utilitarian age it is very hard to understand the purpose of the hermit life. We think of Cuthbert, a gifted evangelist and teacher, cutting himself off from his fellow creatures, denying himself all the good things of this world. And yet the Celtic church, with all its love for creation and life, had no difficulty in accepting this ministry. I think the only way of understanding it is to see the ministry as representative. The Celtic church knew that prayer and devotion to God had to be at the heart of its life if it was to witness to God effectively. The hermit was, to some degree, living out this life for the sake of the community and, indeed, for the sake of the wider community. The hermit provided a kind of anchor for a church which could easily have become overbusy, and which was no doubt tempted by materialism in much the same ways that the church is today. It is interesting to read about Fursey (see Chapter 9), who became immensely popular when he preached in Ireland. Bede tells us that 'he could no longer endure the crowds that thronged him', so he abandoned all he possessed, including his ministry, left Ireland and went to East Anglia. Here he built a monastery, but once again, in the face of rising success, he withdrew and lived the rest of his life as a hermit.

The church today would do well to consider this vital aspect of the life of the Celtic church. We all too easily give in to the seduction of busyness, measuring our value by our usefulness rather than our being. During the 1990s I used to visit the late Brother Ramon, a Franciscan monk who had once travelled extensively around the land, preaching and teaching, but latterly felt called to the hermit life. I visited him in his small hut just beyond the kitchen garden at Glasshampton Monastery in Worcestershire. At the time I knew him, I was travelling a fair bit in the UK and overseas, and there was something immensely reassuring to know that Ramon was there, a human fixed point of prayer and devotion on the lookout in his spiritual watchtower. Brother Ramon, and other hermits like him, are a kind of countercultural movement, offering an alternative way of living to the relentless busyness of so much of our church life. Why do we consider it to be of greater value to have our bishops and clergy attending committees and meetings throughout Lent rather than spending six weeks in contemplative prayer? The Celtic attitude, illustrated so aptly by the life of the hermit, deeply challenges our values.

All kinds of praying

The Celtic hermit would have engaged in praying of all kinds. There were times of aggressive (and probably noisy) battle prayer when the hermits engaged forces of darkness in their praying (as we shall see in Chapter 3). But they also knew the prayer of silence and stillness, which was the foundation of the contemplative life, so treasured by the Celtic church.

The hermit was never an isolated figure. He or she was part of the monastic community. Cuthbert, therefore, when he was on Farne Island, was still seen to be very much part of the community. In the monastic communities, there was a regular rhythm of prayer and worship. Early on, Aidan set up a pattern of prayer and worship on Lindisfarne that became an easy-to-follow example for all. Bede writes, 'Many devout men and women of that day were inspired to follow his example, and adopted the practice of fasting until None on Wednesdays and Fridays throughout the year, except during the fifty days after Easter.'[3] They clearly saw themselves as having an intercessory responsibility for the nation. After a victory against the ever-threatening Penda, King Oswy gave twelve grants of land where, as expressed by Bede, 'heavenly warfare was to take the place of earthly'. This land became the home of a monastic community whose job it was to make constant intercession for the peace of the nation. To turn a battle site into a place of prayer was typical of the Celtic desire to heal the land, turning darkness to light.

The Celtic church seems to have been at ease with formal prayer, and they kept the offices in their communities, but we have many reports of more spontaneous charismatic prayer. One Epiphany, Cuthbert found himself with two brothers on an island off the coast of Scotland. The weather turned bad and they could not get off the island. With no food or water, they realised that the situation was serious. Bede relates Cuthbert's wonderful response to the crisis:

'Why do we remain listless and unresourceful?' he asked. 'We ought to be thinking over every possible way of saving ourselves. The land is bleak with snow, clouds lour in the sky, there is a gale raging and the sea is a fury of waves, we are dying of hunger and there is no chance of human aid. Then let us storm Heaven with our prayers, asking that the same Lord who parted the Red Sea and fed His people in the desert take pity on us in our peril.'[4]

The storms that caused the waves to pound on the rocks caused Cuthbert to stir to prayer. I can imagine him standing in the waves and crying out his prayers, with his great voice being carried on the gales to heaven. This wind-inspired storming of heaven is truly charismatic prayer! Needless to say, it was not long before they found food, and then the storm settled and they made for home.

Patrick's fervent prayers, too, must have had a lot of energy behind them. Prayer was often quite physical. People would pray as they walked. Crossing yourself was a regular part of prayer, as was the drawing of an imaginary circle around you in one of the encircling prayers. Some prayer seems to have been very energetic.

Much of the prayer of the Celtic church would have been spontaneous but, in time, certain prayers became part of church and community rituals, and it is these that were passed down the generations to be gathered in Alexander Carmichael's *Carmina Gadelica* (see Chapter 13 for more on this collection). Even a brief study of these prayers reveals a great respect for words that challenges the wordiness of some church prayers today, both written and extempore. Many of the Celtic prayers are beautifully and poetically written and are designed to stir the soul and touch the heart. With the Celtic love for creation, many connect with the seasons and with all the various aspects of life in God's created order. Celtic Christians found it as natural to pray during the milking of the cow as they did to pray in church. In fact, it was vital to feel at ease in praying while doing such mundane things as milking your cow, because, if you could not do that, your spiritual and earthly worlds were becoming far too separate. Thus there are prayers for getting up in the morning, for washing and dressing, for working, for resting, for meeting friends, for eating, for tidying the house, for undressing, for going to bed. In this way the Celtic church was returning to our Jewish roots, for in Jewish spirituality there has always been a strong earthiness in prayer. David Adam's book *Power Lines*[5] is an excellent example of prayers that connect with modern-day work.

Some evangelicals will find the references to the saints difficult in Celtic prayers, but we need to remember how very important the sense of community was to the Celt. As in Jewish tradition, the community always included those loved ones who had died and for whom life had not ended but simply changed. Mary, Brigid and the archangel Michael are particularly popular in prayers. They all have heavenly tasks to assist our work on earth.

Celtic prayer is always deeply trinitarian. A prayer will often involve all three members of the Trinity (see the prayer at the end of this chapter as an example). Coming into the presence of God in prayer meant coming into the presence of all the members of the Trinity, and the reference to the Three in prayer was deeply reassuring, as the person praying would be made to think of the harmony and unity of the Trinity.

It is sad that, down the ages, different ways of praying have become identified with different churchmanships and denominations. It is my conviction that God is wanting now to break into all of this, so that we can be a united church again, enjoying the fullness of prayer with 'all kinds of praying'.

Bible reading

Mark 1:32–39: Jesus sets the pattern of finding a desert place for prayer in the face of many demands on his time.

Application

1. How do you feel about contemplative, silent prayer? Is it your natural way of praying? Think about those times when Jesus went to a desert place for peace and quiet. Try spending some time today in stillness.
2. What has been your experience of charismatic prayer? Have you engaged in 'heaven-storming' prayer? Next time it is a windy day, why not go out for a walk and pray as the wind stirs you. Feel the moving of the Spirit in you as you pray.
3. You might like to investigate some other Celtic forms of prayer that make use of symbols—try shells, stones, paintings and so on.

Prayer

Before a time of intercession:

Father, in heaven, Jesus came to you at the dawning of the day
in a desert place to be still;
Send stillness to my heart now.

Jesus, you intercede for me at the right hand of the Father;
Help me now to open my heart, mind, body and spirit to you.

Spirit, you are the wind from heaven, that shook the upper
room;
Come to me now, come as gentle breath, come as mighty wind.

Blessed Three,
I come in humility
I come by grace
I come with confidence
I pray in your name
Father, Son and Holy Spirit.

⊕

Spiritual battle

Illtyd

Many would regard Illtyd as the founder of the Welsh church. He was born around AD425 and was apparently a Breton, though some traditions say that he was born near Brecon in Wales. We are informed by one writer that he was by descent a 'most wise Magus Druid and a fore-knower of future events'. He was also extremely intelligent and excellent in rhetoric, maths and philosophy. After his conversion he became a very fine Old and New Testament scholar. But his early passion seems to have been for fighting. He was a Celtic warrior through and through, and legend has it that he was one of King Arthur's knights. He certainly fought for the Celts against the Saxons and, by all accounts, was a devoted and courageous warrior.

His name comes from the Latin phrase *Ille ab omni crimine tutus*, meaning 'the one safe from all evil'. His name was indeed prophetic, for Illtyd was soon to be fighting not against flesh and blood but against principalities and powers of evil. The story goes that he moved from Arthur's army to Glamorgan to fight for King Paulinus. Paulinus was so impressed by Illtyd that he made him chief over his army. On one occasion, Illtyd took some of his soldiers hunting in a forest and, for some reason, the soldiers came across a small hut in the forest that was occupied by an old hermit. The hermit, Cadoc, was living a quiet life after many years of Christian service in Ireland, Scotland, England and Wales, where he had founded a number of monasteries. But all this meant nothing to the pagan soldiers, who forced the hermit to cook them a meal and then delighted in taunting the old man, telling obscene stories and jokes in an attempt to upset him. Eventually Illtyd turned up and was appalled to see the way his soldiers were treating Cadoc. He drove them out of the old man's hut and fell on his knees, begging forgiveness. Illtyd knew he was forgiven as the old man embraced him, and he went back to the palace.

During that night, Illtyd began to reflect on his life and the contrast with Cadoc's life. Eventually he fell asleep and dreamed that an angel came to him and said, 'Until now you have been a knight serving mortal kings; from now on I want you to be a knight in the service of an immortal king, the king of all kings.' When he awoke in the morning, he was in no doubt that he now wanted to fight in God's army against the dark powers of Satan, and no longer fight against other men. So he took off his armour and sword, then crept from the palace and walked to the coast, where he found a sheltered valley near the beach. Here he embarked on a hermit life as he built himself a hut and spent long hours in prayer, battling with the powers of darkness. It was not long before others joined him, including the king's own son, whom Illtyd educated. In time, this little community grew into a large monastic school called Llaniltud Fawr, a monastery that trained David, Samson, Gildas and many other evangelists and teachers who ministered in Wales and beyond. Illtyd died in AD505.

The world of demons and angels has always been very real to the Celtic church. The Celtic view of creation was that it is essentially good and benevolent. However, it was seen as being invaded and menaced by evil spirits. Celtic Christians were aware of these spirit beings, not usually because they saw them with their physical eyesight but because they had such an open imagination. They were able to see what Father Noel Dermot O'Donoghue calls the 'imaginal world', the world that is perceived through intuitive awareness rather than the one that is experienced through scientifically verifiable senses. One of the gifts of the Spirit identified by Paul in 1 Corinthians 12 is that of the discerning of spirits. It is a gift that the church today finds hard to use because, on the whole, we have not been used to operating in this way, and we have a deep suspicion of anything that is too subjective. But the Celtic church saw such gifts as being not only useful but indeed vital for its life and ministry. It is very important for the church in the post-Enlightenment era into which we are entering to become familiar with the Celtic church's understanding of spirits.

Noel Dermot O'Donoghue writes, 'It is because we have lost the faculty of atunement to the region these beings inhabit that we are all too easily persuaded by certain scholars that these beings are no more than imaginary or mythical.'[1] Increasingly, the Christian church in the West is becoming open to the reality of the angel/demon realm, and this faculty of atunement, which has always been so strong in the intuitive Celtic church, is being treated with less disdain. Of course, in many parts of the world where the church is growing rapidly, there is a relaxed acceptance of the angel/demon region, and they find our scepticism very strange. Bishop Graham Dow, in his helpful booklet on deliverance ministry, comments:

It is only the so-called developed Western countries which have difficulty with belief in evil spirits. The majority of the world is quite used to understanding them as part of reality. The question there is not 'Do they exist?' but 'Who has power over them?' The dean of a Chinese

theological college visiting the diocese of Coventry in a Mission in
Partnership exercise in 1988 roared with laughter when I told him that
most English clergy do not believe in evil spirits. We should be open to
the possibility that the rest of the world is right in its perception of the
way things are. [2]

It is all too easy to read about this dimension of early Celtic
literature and regard the stories of angels and demons as a quaint
fantasy for the past. For the Celtic saints, as for many Christians
in the developing world today, this region is one of reality, not
fantasy, and a proper appreciation of spiritual warfare is essential
for understanding Celtic Christian spirituality.

If we look at the life of Cuthbert we find a man for whom the
battle was very real. While he was at Melrose, he was frequently out
on preaching trips. On one such occasion, a huge crowd gathered
to hear him, and while he was speaking Cuthbert became aware
that 'the ancient enemy, the devil, was present, come to hinder
his work of salvation'. Bede tells us that Cuthbert then exhorted
the crowd to be on their guard against the devil's attacks, for,
Cuthbert explained, 'he has a thousand crafty ways of harming
you'. Cuthbert was under no illusion that the enemy was real and
dangerous, but he was also utterly confident of the power of God.
There was no dualism in his thinking.

As Cuthbert continued to preach, the devil sent down 'mock
fire' to a nearby house. Bede relates:

Sheets of flame, fanned by the wind, seemed to sweep through the whole
village, and the noise of their crackling rent the air. Cuthbert managed,
with outstretched arms, to restrain a few of the villagers, but the rest,
almost the whole crowd, leaped up and vied with each other in throwing
water on the flames. But real water has no effect on phantom fire, and
the blaze raged on, until through Cuthbert's prayers the father of lies
fled, taking his false fire with him into the empty air. [3]

The crowd were naturally astonished but also felt ashamed that they did not trust Cuthbert, who was encouraging them to pray rather than pour water on the phantom flames. Bede tells us that the crowd then appreciated that 'the devil did not cease for even an hour in his warfare against man's salvation'. Such stories of phantom fire may seem strange to many of us in the West, but they are not uncommon in various parts of the world today, especially where there is an exceptionally powerful outpouring of the Holy Spirit. There is no doubt that God was working most powerfully through Cuthbert, and attacks such as this on his evangelistic preaching were expected. But Cuthbert takes it all in his stride, and Bede records it all in a fairly matter-of-fact sort of way. There is no attempt to sensationalise the story in the way that is done by some Christian writers today who tell stories of spiritual combat. This kind of warfare was seen as normal for those who wanted to follow Christ.

Cuthbert also knew the fierceness of the battle when he was alone on Farne Island. This was probably a far harder contest, when he was on his own in a place of such vulnerability. Bede tells us that before going to Farne Island, Cuthbert lived in solitude in the outer precincts of the Lindisfarne monastery. We know that he spent some time on 'Cuddy's Isle'.

Not till he first gained victory over our invisible enemy by solitary prayer and fasting did he take it on himself to seek out a remote battlefield farther away from his fellow man… The Farne lies a few miles to the south-east of Lindisfarne, cut off on the landward side by very deep water and facing, on the other side, out towards the limitless ocean. The island was haunted by devils; Cuthbert was the first man brave enough to live there alone. At the entry of our soldier of Christ armed with 'the helmet of salvation, the shield of faith and the sword of the spirit which is the word of God', the devil fled and his host of allies with him. [4]

Contamination and consecration

With the strong influence of the Desert Fathers, the Celtic church saw these wilderness areas as places of deep spiritual conflict. The precedent for this was our Lord's 40-day fast in the wilderness. In the Judean desert Jesus fasted and prayed and was tempted by the devil. Cuthbert was following his master into the desert to wrestle, fight and pray. As we see from Bede, Farne Island was a frightening place. It presumably had something of the feel of a graveyard on a dark night, and no one before Cuthbert had dared go there alone. But why was this island so very infested with demons? Why should some places be particularly infected? Perhaps it had been the place of pagan sacrifices. Perhaps dark deeds of cursing had taken place here. We shall probably never know, but as far as the Celtic church was concerned this island was a very dark place until Cuthbert cleansed it. Thereafter it became a hallowed place.

When we put together the Celtic love for creation and their extraordinary spiritual perceptiveness and understanding of the spirit realm, we find a view of the land that is very interesting. Land was viewed as good, but it could be contaminated. We get an insight into this idea in the story of Cedd, who was asked by Ethelwald, son of King Oswald, to found a monastery to which he could come and pray and where his body could be buried. Cedd's job was first of all to find a good site for a monastery. In today's way of thinking, we would probably look for a site with good amenities and with easy access, but this was not the way Cedd thought.

Cedd chose a site for the monastery among some high and remote hills, which seemed more suitable for the dens of robbers and haunts of wild beasts than for human habitation. His purpose in this was to fulfil the prophecy of Isaiah, in the habitation of dragons, where each lay, shall be grass, with reeds and rushes, so that the fruits of good works might spring up where formerly lived only wild beasts, or men who lived like wild beasts.[5]

Cedd's wish was to see the land redeemed as a symbol of God redeeming humankind. But he discerned that this particular area of land was not only naturally harsh; there was a supernatural discomfort about the place brought about by 'earlier crimes'. We are not told what these were, but clearly some kind of human sin had contaminated the land, which now had to be cleansed by the Christian priestly ministry of blessing the land. Cedd decided to give the whole of Lent over to fasting and praying on the site to cleanse it. He fasted till sunset every day except Sunday, which was always a feast day. In fact, ten days before Easter he was called away on some urgent business by the king, so, rather than let the fast be thwarted, Cedd asked his brother Cynibil to take over. By Easter the fast was complete, the land was considered clean and blessed, and here the monastery of Lastingham was established.

It is interesting to see how this attitude to the land is being renewed today. Many people are becoming aware of real geographical locations of both spiritual darkness and spiritual light. Quite often the darkness is connected with occult activity or some kind of human injustice that was committed centuries ago but nonetheless still seems to be infecting the ground. Confession and prayer are proving effective ways of changing the atmosphere. Russ Parker, in his excellent book *Healing Wounded History*, explores this phenomenon in some detail and writes about the need to 'heal the land', a term taken from 2 Chronicles 7:14. He writes, 'Healing the land brings together the strands of unhealed history and the locations where such stories continue to exert a shaping of the people living there.'[6] In a section called 'The power of holy places and the pain of hurting places', he writes that we need

... to know where the equivalent of the blood of Abel cries out from the ground (Genesis 4:10) for recognition and healing. Yet this is only one aspect of the reconciliation and healing that is needed. Not only must we deal with the sins of our forebears and their consequences upon others and ourselves—we must find ways of reconnecting with the land for our

own identity and growth. Peter Berg calls this bioregionalism, *by which he means that each earth region has its own unique, interdependent regional culture and identity and that we must learn to become native to our own place and be aware of our ecological relationships which operate within it.*[7]

I am sure the early Celtic Christian communities would have been highly aware of this sacramental duty to listen to the story of the land and to bless and heal it, and deliver it from oppressive powers, as well as celebrating its goodness. As we shall see later, this is very closely connected to their love for creation.

Warfare and protection

With its keen sense of awareness of good and evil in the world, the Celtic church engaged actively not only in prayers of blessing but also in prayers of protection. Patrick was very aware of the need for protection following a sinister and frightening dream that he records in his *Confession*:

But the same night while I was sleeping and Satan greatly tempted me, in a way which I shall remember as long as I am in this body. And he fell upon me like a huge rock, and I had no power in my limbs, save that it came to me, into my mind, that I should call out 'Helias'. And in that moment I saw the sun rise in the heaven; and while I was crying out 'Helias' with all my might, behold the splendour of that sun fell upon me, and at once removed the weight from me. And I believe I was aided by Christ my Lord, and His Spirit was then crying out for me.[8]

The experience, for Patrick, left him in no doubt that the spiritual battle was real. It also left him in no doubt of the power of Christ and the Holy Spirit.

The story is recorded that Patrick was involved in a Mount

Carmel-type contest with the pagan druids and King of Tara, a centre of witchcraft and darkness. After this victorious encounter Patrick is said to have written the famous 'St Patrick's Breastplate'. Whether or not he was the author, the prayer is certainly early and is consistent with Patrick's life and ministry. It is a glorious prayer that rejoices in the power of the Holy Trinity to protect us:

I arise today
Through a mighty strength, the invocation of the Trinity,
Through belief in the threeness,
Through confession of the oneness of the Creator of Creation.[9]

The whole prayer is quite wonderful and includes some fairly specific prayers of protection against 'Satan's spells and wiles', as well as references to such things as 'wizard's evil craft', 'poisoned shaft' and other well-known devices used by those involved in witchcraft to attack Christians. Right after this rather horrendous part of the prayer comes the beautiful Christ-centred prayer that rises majestically as a triumphant peak:

Christ be with me, Christ within me,
Christ behind me, Christ before me,
Christ beside me, Christ to win me,
Christ to comfort and restore me.
Christ beneath me, Christ above me,
Christ in quiet, Christ in danger,
Christ in hearts of all that love me,
Christ in mouth of friend and stranger.
C.F. ALEXANDER'S VERSION

Such a prayer as Patrick's was often called a *lorica* prayer, which means 'breastplate', picking up the imagery used by Paul in Ephesians 6:14. There are many of these prayers in the *Carmina Gadelica*, and they reflect the Celtic church's awareness of our need for protection. Some of them took the form of 'encompassing' or 'encircling' prayers, where the index finger of the right hand would be extended and you would draw an imaginary circle around you while you prayed a prayer of protection. In the case of Patrick's prayer above, you would see in your mind's eye the protection of Christ around, above, beneath and within you. The encircling prayer is often called a *caim* and is becoming increasingly popular today. David Adam, who has written a number of *caim* prayers, comments, 'This was no magic, it was no attempt to manipulate God. It was a reminder by action that we are always surrounded by God, he is our encompasser, our encircler.'[10]

We don't have to look far to see the reality of evil in our world today. When we see graphic and horrific details from war-torn lands or the disfigured bodies of those suffering famine, and when we have in our own land terrible violence on the streets, we know that there is a deep darkness at work in the world. As we study the Celtic church, we discover a community of Christian people who took this darkness seriously. They developed very effective ways of protecting themselves from its influence. Not only that but they were also extremely effective in delivering people and land from the influences of evil. They would be very puzzled by the liberal dismissal of a personal devil. Equally, they would feel ill at ease with charismatic spiritual 'hype' and forms of spiritual warfare that all too easily pander to our own needs for power. Rather, with their usual combination of humility and confidence, and with their well-earthed spirituality, the Celtic church developed a well-integrated and thoroughly biblical response to the presence of evil in this world.

Bible reading

Ephesians 6:10–20: Paul gives practical advice on how to resist the devil.

Application

1. What is your view of spiritual warfare? How does the Celtic approach to evil compare with your own view?
2. Have you ever had any experiences like Patrick's? Have you been to places that feel 'spooky'? Do you know why they seem like this? Have you been to places that have a good atmosphere and feel blessed? Why do you think they feel good?
3. Try to find the time to take a walk in your neighbourhood, asking the Holy Spirit to give you a gift of discernment, so that you can be open to sensing where there are good places to bless and bad places that you can pray about. Be open to the possibility of God taking you into a season of prayer and fasting for unhappy places in your neighbourhood, where the land needs healing.

Prayer

In the midst of dark powers
We magnify the greatness of heaven

In the midst of foul deeds
We magnify the greatness of heaven

In the midst of fearful thoughts
We magnify the greatness of heaven

In the midst of a blighted land
We magnify the greatness of heaven

In our time of need
We magnify the greatness of heaven

We praise you, Lord of earth and heaven
We magnify you on earth as in heaven.[11]

Ministry of women

Brigid

In the middle of the fifth century, during the early days of the Christian mission in Ireland, a girl was born who was to become one of the greatest saints in the Celtic church. Historical facts about her life are rare but there are accounts which tell us that her father was Dubtach, the King of Leinster. Her mother was a Christian called Brocseach, who was a bondswoman of the king. Shortly before her child was born, the king sold Brocseach to a druid priest. So it was that Brigid (also known as Brigit, Bridget and Bride) was born to a Christian mother in a pagan household. There seems to have been something special about Brigid from her earliest days. She was apparently baptised by Patrick, who no doubt discerned the call of God on her life.

Some years later, the king decided to have his daughter back in the palace, but he soon regretted it because Brigid had the annoying habit of constantly giving away food and goods from the palace to the poor! By the time Brigid was 14, Dubtach could stand it no longer, so he decided to marry her off to a nobleman nearby. She stubbornly refused and instead opted to become a nun. It seems that the king had no objection to this, and so the young Brigid embarked on a remarkable ministry.

Her strong-willed and buoyant personality soon led her to found her own community. She needed to find some land for this, so she appealed to the local chief for a small plot. He refused. Characteristically, Brigid persevered, eventually getting him to agree to give her a piece of land that was no bigger than the size of her cloak. The chief was astonished to find that when Brigid laid her cloak on the grass, it grew until it covered the whole of the Curragh, the grassy plain to the east of Kildare! Here was founded one of the most famous communities in Ireland, and Brigid became the abbess. Kildare was famed for its magical oak trees, which were very special to the druids, but Brigid's community turned it into a centre where Christ was exalted, and the light of the gospel shone from the community to the pagan world around it. Brigid lit a fire at the centre of the community as a sign of this light. Only women were allowed to tend the fire, and it remained alight for a thousand years, until the dissolution of the monasteries.

Brigid remained based at the same community for the rest of her life and died around AD524 at the age of 70. Later her remains were taken to be placed alongside Patrick's in Downpatrick. The people of Ireland have traditionally respected Patrick and Brigid as their two greatest evangelists.

There were a number of fundamental differences between Celtic society and other European societies, and one of these was in the attitude to women. Peter Beresford Ellis writes:

The status of women in Celtic society and their social prominence has been found remarkable by many scholars. The female had a unique place in the Celtic world compared with other civilisations. She was regarded equally and could be elected as chief; she could, and did, lead her tribe as military commander—as the Icenian Boudicca did in 60AD. Celtic women enjoyed an equality of rights which would have been envied by their Roman sisters. [1]

In Roman society, when a woman married, she effectively became a belonging of the man's family, along with all her goods. By law, she could own no property. In Celtic society, the woman very much retained her identity and there was no sense that the husband owned her or her belongings. A Celtic woman continued personally to own anything she brought into the marriage, and the husband had no rights over her property. Nora Chadwick, in *The Celts*, informs us that 'an interesting feature of Pictish institutions was inheritance through the female'. [2] All this, of course, needs to be seen in the context of the close community in which the Celts lived. The tribe was a close-knit family, in which household duties were shared, both parents took responsibility for raising the children and both parents were free to follow their work, leaving the children safe in the care of the tribe. Perhaps the community nature of Celtic life was the key that enabled women to enjoy a freedom denied them in other, more individualistic cultures.

It was therefore inevitable that the emerging Christian church would take this positive attitude to women into their community life. Thus there was no problem with women like Brigid, Hilda, Ebba, Ethelburga and others exercising leadership roles in their communities. Again, because there was a strong sense of equality within the community, the rights of women do not seem to have been an issue. Brigid was clearly well respected and accepted in her role as abbess of her community in Kildare. This community contained both men and women and, as Shirley Toulson points out, as a manager 'Brigid must have shown the organising ability, energy and common sense of Teresa of Avila, who also combined worldly wisdom with spiritual insights'.[3]

Mary Calvert, writing about Brigid, informs us, 'Brigid needed priests to perform the offices which no woman was allowed to... She selected Conleath to be the bishop who "in episcopal dignity" would govern with her, but as to who actually ruled the abbey, there was never any real doubt!'[4]

I have not yet discovered anything in early Celtic literature to tell us if there was any debate about whether leaders like Brigid were seeking ordination. However, one legendary tale does suggest that there were some who would have been very comfortable with the idea of Brigid being not only a priest, but a bishop. Christopher Bamford and William Parker Marsh record for us the story of her visit to Telcha Mide with a number of other women, for a service of 'taking the veil' led by Bishop Mel. During the course of the ceremony, a strange phenomenon took place:

A fiery pillar rose from her head to the roof-ridge of the church. Then said Bishop Mel: 'Come, O holy Brigid, that a veil may be sained on thy head before the other virgins.'

It came to pass then, through the grace of the Holy Ghost, that the form of ordaining a Bishop was read over Brigid. Mac-Caille said that a bishop's order should not be conferred on a woman.

Said Bishop Mel: 'No power have I in this matter. That dignity hath been given by God unto Brigid, beyond every woman.' Wherefore the men of Ireland from that time to this give episcopal honour to Brigid's successor.[5]

Whatever we make of stories like this, it tells us that there existed a tradition that deeply respected Brigid and would have had no objection if heaven had decided to consecrate her as a bishop.

Hilda of Whitby

Brigid's community in Ireland must have been an inspiration to Hilda, who is a much-loved Celtic saint in England. Hilda was a rather different personality from Brigid. The impression of Brigid is that she had a lot of fight in her and was a leader because she was strong-willed and determined, characteristics that God wonderfully used at Kildare. Hilda was more of an intellectual and a diplomat. Like Brigid, she was born into a royal family. She was the daughter of Hereric, nephew to King Edwin. Her mother was Breguswith, who had a significant dream one night when Hilda was an infant. In this dream, Hereric was suddenly taken away from her and, although she searched everywhere for him, she could not find him. But at the end of her searching, she did find something quite unexpected. Bede tells us, 'She discovered a most valuable jewel under her garments; and as she looked closely, it emitted such a brilliant light that all Britain was lit by its splendour.'⁶ Breguswith lost her husband shortly afterwards when he was poisoned in a political intrigue, but she had discovered a jewel, which was her daughter, and the dream was certainly prophetic, for Hilda became a jewel that brightened the whole of Britain.

Hilda was baptised by Bishop Paulinus in AD627 when she was 13 years old. Bede tells us that her life neatly fitted into two parts: she spent 33 years 'most nobly in secular occupations', followed by 33 years in the monastic life. It was Aidan who encouraged her into the latter ministry, no doubt influenced by the way that women's ministry had been developed in the communities in Ireland where he had come from. Aidan had already appointed Ebba to found a convent at Coldingham, near Berwick, in about 640. Her niece, Elfleda, also had a very distinguished ministry and she eventually became abbess at Whitby. Hilda was deeply influenced by the way of life developed by Aidan on Lindisfarne. She had thought of moving to France, but Aidan persuaded her to exercise her ministry in Britain. She initially established a new monastery on the north side of the Wear, then moved on to lead the community for men and women at Hartlepool. She had not long been there when she moved, with characteristic Celtic restlessness, to form another community, this time at Tadcaster. She remained in Tadcaster until she founded the monastery for which she became famous. This was at a place called Streanaeshalch, which we now call Whitby. Bede writes of her ministry here:

She established the same regular life as in her former monastery, and taught the observance of righteousness, mercy, purity, and other virtues, but especially of peace and charity. After the example of the primitive Church, no one there was rich, no one was needy, for everything was held in communion, and nothing was considered to be anyone's personal property. So great was her prudence that not only ordinary folk, but kings and princes used to come and ask her advice in their difficulties and take it. Those under her direction were required to make a thorough study of the Scriptures and occupy themselves in good works, to such good effect that many were found fitted for Holy Orders and the service of God's altar.[7]

It was clearly an extraordinary community, constantly training men and women for ministry. Five men from this monastery, including John of Beverley, became bishops. But the clerics were deemed no more important than the lay people. It was at Whitby that the famous Synod was held in AD664 to determine the future direction of the British church. We get the impression that at this tense conference Hilda was very much involved in a conciliatory way, trying to hold the two groups, Roman and Celtic, together. But it must have saddened her deeply to see the decision go to the Romans, for she was very much of the Celtic persuasion. She must also have had grave misgivings about the Roman view of women, which was far more oppressive than the Celtic attitude.

Towards the end of her life Hilda became very ill and she was

racked by a fever for six years. Despite the fact that stories of miraculous healings abounded all around her, Hilda was not cured of
her physical ailment, but she bore it courageously and was a great
example to others in the community. Eventually, on 17 November
680, Hilda, to use the words of Bede, 'joyfully welcomed death'.
The evening she died, in a new monastery a few miles away that
she had only recently founded, a nun named Begu was sleeping in
her dormitory when she heard the sound of a bell, the bell that was
rung when someone died. She opened her eyes and saw a vision
of the roof opening and a great light flooding into the room. When
she gazed into this light, she saw the soul of Hilda being taken up
into heaven by several angels.[8]

The Celtic church and human sexuality

We find in the Celtic church a strong community context in
which men and women worked happily together. Many monastic
communities contained both men and women, and many engaged
in close and meaningful relationships with one another, apparently
free from the Roman fear that any such friendships would sooner
or later degenerate into lustful ways. Thus Brigid and Conleath,
Aidan and Hilda, Cuthbert and Aelfflaed could all enjoy useful and
affectionate working relationships. It seems that the Celtic creation-
affirming approach to life helped in this. The Roman church, influenced by the post-Augustinian negative view of human nature as
depraved, saw a need to guard against its weaknesses. But the
Celtic church always took a more positive view of human nature,
and in many ways seemed to be much more at ease with human
sexuality.

Patrick, in his *Confession*, gives us an insight into his attitude
to women and to his sexuality. Noel Dermot O'Donoghue writes
most movingly about this in his book on Patrick, entitled *Aristocracy
of Soul*. He devotes a chapter of this book to exploring a little para-

graph towards the end of the *Confession*, where Patrick writes about a 'blessed Scottic maiden, nobly born, very beautiful, of adult age', whom Patrick baptised. She is given no name, so O'Donoghue calls her Pulcherrima, the word Patrick used to describe how beautiful this maiden was. O'Donoghue ponders on why Patrick mentions this young woman. Was he troubled by her very attractive presence? Was he tempted sexually? He may have been tempted, but it seems to O'Donoghue that there is something else happening here, and it is the discovery by Patrick of a gift of femininity to the church. For Pulcherrima is giving herself as a virgin to service in the church. She is voluntarily choosing not to use her beauty for other ends. Yet this is not a denial of her beauty: she is not going to hide it. It is a gift for the church. O'Donoghue concludes that in writing as he does:

[Patrick] is deeply and sensitively open to women and womanhood, and has in himself a certain vulnerability, if not a susceptibility, which nevertheless does not take refuge in grim and pretentious asceticism, nor yet in that neurotic fear of and contempt for the feminine which has entered so deeply into the attitudes and structures of the Christian Church in its main manifestations. In this respect he is a complete man.[9]

My impression is that the Celtic church had a wonderfully whole attitude to human sexuality, affirming male and female and finding both naturally expressed in the lives of their community. Interestingly, despite their relatively radical approach to women's ministry, this did not prevent the Celtic church from affirming the domestic work of women. Brigid, for all her work of leadership in Christian ministry, is remembered in tradition for her 'motherliness'. Many Celtic prayers in the home involve invocations to Brigid. Along with Mary the mother of Jesus, she is frequently remembered in Celtic domestic prayers. In fact, this dimension of Brigid's character was so important that, in time, a legend arose that she was the midwife and wet-nurse present at the birth of Christ. Thus we have prayers such as:

I am under the shielding
  Of good Brigit each day;
I am under the shielding
  Of good Brigit each night.

I am under the keeping
  Of the nurse of Mary,
Each early and late,
  Every dark, every light.

Brigit is my companion-woman,
  Brigit is my maker of song.
Brigit is my helping woman,
  My choicest of women, my woman of guidance.[10]

No doubt this imagery was connected with the sense that she was a midwife to the church in Ireland. But in the devotion to Brigid, the Celtic church founded a model of one who could be both motherly and managerial. The two were not mutually exclusive or divided as they had become in other forms of European Christianity.

We find in the Celtic church, then, an impressive acceptance of the feminine. It is desperately sad to recognise how this was lost after the Synod of Whitby. Had we been allowed to pursue the natural faith that the Spirit of God first breathed upon this land, which contained a far more just attitude to women than was experienced in the church elsewhere, then our shameful history of repression of women may not have developed and there would have been no need for the over-reaction of extreme forms of feminism that are, for some, the only way they know how to cry for justice. We would also have had a far healthier attitude to sexuality generally, affirming the masculine and feminine within ourselves and within our communities.

Bible reading

Luke 24:1–12: The women are given the honour of being the first witnesses to the resurrection of Jesus.

Application

1. What is the attitude to women in your church? Has the ministry of women been encouraged? If not, what discourages it? Spend a bit of time speaking to the Lord about this and try to hear what his feelings are.
2. Reflect on how you feel about your own sexuality. Do you feel affirmed by God in your femininity/masculinity? Do you feel affirmed in the community of the church?
3. Spend some time meditating on Brigid's or Hilda's community. Allow the Holy Spirit to bless your imagination as you see in your mind's eye this community bustling with life. After imagining it for a while, compare it with your church. Are there aspects of the Celtic community that you would like to see in your church?

Prayer

May I abide in Christ.
May the brightness He gave Brigid lie on me.
May the delight He gave Brigid lie on me.
May the blossom He gave Brigid lie on me.
May the healings He gave Brigid lie on me.
May the calmness He gave Brigid lie on me.[11]

⊕

— 5 —

Wild Goose

Brendan

Brendan was born around AD486 near Tralee in Ireland and he lived to be over 90 years old. The Christianity that Patrick and Brigid had spread throughout Ireland meant that almost every local community had become connected with a monastic settlement. It was clear that Brendan had a special calling on his life. Before he was born, Brendan's mother dreamed that her breast was full of pure gold. On the night of his birth, Erc, the local bishop, saw the village 'all in one great blaze' with angels in shining white garments all around it. When he realised that they were heralding the birth of this special child, Erc took great care of him, teaching him the Bible as he grew up. In due course Brendan was ordained and became a monk.

He became one of the 'Twelve Apostles of Ireland', as they were called. These were twelve men who were pupils of Finian of Clonard. It was the custom for Christian leaders to choose twelve disciples, following the pattern of Jesus. They would teach these twelve, training them for Christian service. Finian's twelve included not only Brendan but also Ciaran of Clonmacnoise, Brendan of Birr, and the famous Columba who was eventually to go to Iona.

Brendan became Abbot of Clonfert, a large monastery in central Ireland, but there was a restlessness in him and he was deeply infected by the Celtic spirit of adventure. One year, he spent Lent on top of a high mountain at the south-western tip of Ireland, above Bantry Bay, fasting and praying and looking out over the vast Atlantic. He could see the rocks of Skellig Michael, where brave monks lived an austere life in their beehive huts, which still exist today. Brendan was impressed by them but he did not want to stop at an island. He wanted to adventure further, to discover islands beyond the horizon. He sensed the unfurling wings of the Wild Goose, the Celtic symbol of the Holy Spirit, who was urging him to spread his own wings and travel to far-off lands, not only with a desire to spread the gospel but with a mystical quest to seek glimpses of Paradise. He had met travellers before who had encountered such places on earth, and he had become gripped with this longing. So sure was Brendan that this was a call of God that he returned to his community and chose 14 monks to travel with him. He said to them, 'My beloved fellow soldiers in the spiritual war: I beg your help, because my heart is set upon a single desire. If it be God's will, I want to seek out the Island of Promise of which our forefathers have spoken.'

Thus it was that Brendan and his 14 companions built their simple coracle and set out into the Atlantic, allowing the wild wind of the Spirit to take them where it would. The account of their travels is recorded in *The Voyage of Brendan*, which became an immensely popular book in the Middle Ages. It was no doubt highly embellished, but behind the parables and hyperbole we can discover a group of wonderfully open travellers who came upon small island communities of monks, encountered the wonders of icebergs and great whales, and travelled vast distances in their fragile coracle, quite possibly discovering America eight centuries before Christopher Columbus.

According to legend, Brendan did find his island of Paradise but was told not to stay there because he would only spoil it! After several years of travelling, he returned to Ireland. After a very long life, he embarked on his final journey, the journey of death, in 575, requesting that his body be buried at Clonfert, which was now a community numbering some 3000 brothers.

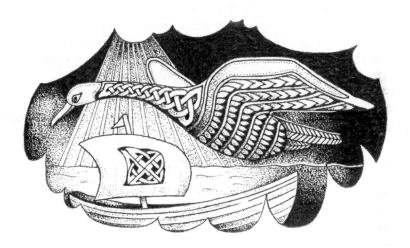

Although *The Voyage of Brendan* is embellished, the great spirit of adventure that was so much part of early Irish Christianity was clearly the inspiration behind this extraordinary journey. There is in the story a delightful integration of a love for creation and a longing for the spiritual reality of Paradise. On one occasion, after sailing for months in the north Atlantic without seeing anything, Brendan and his companions came across an iceberg. It was the first time they had seen one, and did not know that such things existed. Brendan gazed up at it. It was so high that he could hardly see the top, and he could see that it plunged deep into the sea. It was clearly a large iceberg, and they found a tunnel in it that they could sail through. The writer describes it: 'It was the colour of silver and seemed harder than marble. The column itself was of pure crystal.' Brendan was delighted to spend time with the extraordinary crystal island and exhorted his fellow travellers, 'Let us inspect the wonders of God, our Maker.' They spent the whole day inspecting and measuring this phenomenon.[1]

Such a story as this reveals the Celtic travellers' delight in God's creation. This was one of their driving forces. They deeply desired to discover more of the wonders of his creation. They experienced God as wonderful, and the wonders of his creation led them on to the discoveries of the unseen marvels of Paradise.

The Celtic church was very alert to the activity of the Holy Spirit, who was so involved in creation. They chose the symbol of the wild goose to represent the Spirit because, having studied this bird, they saw in it so much of the life and work of the Spirit.

Patrick and the Spirit

Patrick, whose influence was so strong in Ireland, had a deep appreciation of the presence and activity of the Holy Spirit. The Celtic church had close associations with the Eastern church, which has always had a 'high doctrine' of the Holy Spirit. One of the points of dispute between the Eastern and Western churches has been over the inclusion in the Creed of the word *filioque*, which means 'and the Son'. The Western church describes the Spirit as proceeding from the Father *and the Son*. The Eastern Church felt that this wording subordinated the Spirit to the Son and opted for the phrase to read simply, 'proceeding from the Father'. It may seem a doctrinal detail to us today, but experience has shown that the Eastern Orthodox churches have always had a high expectation of the activity and gifts of the Holy Spirit among them. Patrick eagerly picked up this love for the Holy Spirit, which is clear to us in his *Confession*. Noel Dermot O'Donoghue comments:

The Confession of Patrick is animated from beginning to end by the Holy Spirit, who is named as the Spirit (11, 43, 46), the Spirit of God (33), the Spirit of the Living God (11), the Spirit of the Father (20)... A more careful reading of the text shows that the Spirit initiates the whole process of Patrick's conversion and sanctification. [2]

One of the most intimate experiences of the Spirit that Patrick underwent is described in his *Confession*, where he recounts one of his extraordinary dreams:

And again I saw Him praying in me, and He was as it were within my body, and I heard him above me, that is above the inner man, and there He was praying mightily with groanings. And meanwhile I was stupefied and astonished, and pondered who it could be that was praying in me. But at the end of the prayer He spoke as if He were the Spirit. And so I awoke, and remembered that the Apostle says, 'The Spirit helps the infirmities of our prayers. For we know not what we should pray for as we ought; but the Spirit Himself asketh for us with unspeakable groanings'. [3]

This is an excellent insight into Patrick's understanding and experience of the Spirit. It tells us that he had an expectation of the Spirit communicating in his dream life. O'Donoghue, in his commentary, says that this experience informs us that 'the region of dreams has within it pathways along which the Holy Spirit can reach us'. The dream tells us that the Spirit is not a remote, otherworldly or unreachably mystical person of the Trinity. Far from it: the Holy Spirit actually enters the most intimate place of our psyche, the inner world of the unconscious. For Patrick and the Celtic church, the Spirit was the glorious gift of God who visits us intimately and powerfully. In his *Confession* we find this continuous activity of the Spirit, with the charismatic gifts of 1 Corinthians 12 very much present. We find expressions of prophecy, wisdom, knowledge, discerning of spirits and faith, and in Patrick's wider ministry we find the Spirit working in healings and miracles. I have yet to find reference to speaking in tongues or interpretation of tongues in Celtic literature, though it is possible that Patrick's groanings included these gifts, and I think it is very likely that the Celtic church loved to use them. On the whole, the gift of tongues presents difficulties only for those who are confined to a rationalistic view of the activity of God in us. For the intuitive Celt, the idea of a heavenly language coming from the intimacy of our hearts and bypassing the logic of the mind would have been very easy to receive.

The Celtic church practised the ministry of confirmation by its bishops. In the days when the Celtic fire was burning bright, these must have been great events. Bede describes for us one of Cuthbert's confirmations:

Once when this most holy shepherd of the Lord's flock was doing the round of his sheepfolds, he came into a rough mountain area whither many had gathered from the scattered villages to be confirmed. Now there was no church nor even a place in the mountains fit to receive a bishop and his retinue, so the people put up tents for him while for themselves they made huts of felled branches as best they could. Cuthbert preached twice to the milling crowds and brought down the grace of the Holy Ghost by imposition of hands on those newly regenerated in Christ.[4]

Such was the presence of the Spirit at this outdoor confirmation service that a young man with a wasting disease received healing. So the Spirit was seen as coming in power at the confirmation service, and thereafter would be intimately involved with the believer. Once you received the Spirit in this way, you began a life of adventure, open to the leading of the Wild Goose.

Wild Goose and divine restlessness

In some ways, the Holy Spirit would not have had to work too hard on the Celtic peoples because they were natural travellers and explorers. Nonetheless, there was a real cost involved in pulling up roots and venturing forth, often in small rudderless coracles, at the mercy of tides, currents and winds that were used by the Spirit of God to take them to places of God's choice. The cost was reflected in the use of the word 'martyrdom'. The Celtic church identified three kinds of martyrdom. White martyrdom was the leaving of home for the sake of the gospel. Red martyrdom meant dying for the sake of Christ. The early Celtic church seldom experienced red martyrdom until the coming of the Vikings, who often made straight for the Celtic communities in their raids on this country. Visitors to Iona can still go to the bay of martyrs today, the site where 68 monks were slaughtered by Norse raiders in 806. But while there were few red martyrs in the early years, there were thousands of 'green' martyrs. Green martyrdom was primarily to do with a life of confession and penance, which included a voluntary giving up of normal securities. Many therefore felt a sense of calling for white and green martyrdom, and this in part contributed to the desire to leave one's secure home to become what was called a *perigrinatus*, a wanderer for the sake of Christ. Elizabeth Culling writes:

The peregrinati *set out with no particular destination in mind, but wherever they found themselves they preached Christ and sought to live out the gospel. The 'Lives' of the saints frequently state that pilgrimage was undertaken 'for the love of God… for the name of Christ… for the salvation of souls and to attain heaven.'*[5]

This sense of martyrdom, of giving up all for the sake of Christ, is reflected in Brendan's beautiful and touching prayer:

Shall I abandon, O King of Mysteries, the soft comforts of home? Shall I turn my back on my native land, and my face towards the sea?

Shall I put myself wholly at the mercy of God, without silver, without a horse, without fame and honour? Shall I throw myself wholly on the King of kings, without sword and shield, without food and drink, without a bed to lie on?

Shall I say farewell to my beautiful land, placing myself under Christ's yoke? Shall I pour out my heart to him, confessing my manifold sins and begging forgiveness, tears streaming down my cheeks?

Shall I leave the prints of my knees on the sandy beach, a record of my final prayer in my native land? Shall I then suffer every kind of wound that the sea can inflict?

Shall I take my tiny coracle across the wide, sparkling ocean? O King of the Glorious Heaven, shall I go of my own choice upon the sea?

O Christ, will you help me on the wild waves?[6]

The *peregrinati* felt that they were being obedient to Jesus' call to leave home and family and follow him. They were also aware that their Master was one who wandered and never had anywhere to rest his head (Matthew 8:20). He was one who journeyed across barren wastelands and walked on the wild waves. This sense of reckless travelling, brought about by the divine restlessness within, says much to our organised and often far-too-safe Western church. The Celtic church reminds us that we were born to quest and that pilgrimage is at the heart of our Christian discipleship. David Adam explains the title of one of his books, *The Open Gate*, in this way:

As long as we are alive, we are on the move. To become static is to stagnate and die. It is necessary for all living things to move and grow and change. Life is meant to be an adventure; change is a gift that we have to learn to use aright. In Celtic folk-tales a curse that could happen to a person was to enter a field and not to be able to get back out of it. To be stuck in that place for ever. It was seen as a definite curse to be unable to venture or to change. The open gate is the opposite to this. It is the invitation to adventure and to grow, the call to be among the living and vital elements of the world. The open gate is the call to explore new areas of yourself and the world around you.[7]

Not only do we have to learn to adventure, but we also need to know the Celtic simplicity that will let go of the baggage and clutter that weighs us down. Shirley Toulson speaks of the need to let go of our 'trunkfuls of preconceptions, such badly packed, uncomfortable rucksacks of dogma, prejudice and projects'.[8] There is a wildness about the Holy Spirit, who is like the wind that 'blows where it chooses, and you hear the sound of it, but you do not know where it comes from or where it goes' (John 3:8, NRSV). Too many churches have wanted to domesticate the Holy Spirit, keeping this Wild Goose caged and 'safe' by imposing rigid and controlling worship styles on our Sunday worship (whether it be liturgical or 'free'), trapping our meetings with bureaucracy and endless reports, and feeding our people with tragically low expectations of what God can do in and through them.

As we settle into this third millennium AD, the Celtic church of the first millennium wonderfully and joyfully challenges us to learn once again what it means to have a carefree spirit of adventure. The Wild Goose is certainly unfurling its wings over our land once more with renewed vigour in our time. There are signs of spiritual springtime, despite the frost and ice in many parts of our church and society. Now is surely the time to become open again to the Spirit of God who desires to come to the most intimate places of our lives, praying, healing and transforming us, that we may be released to a new sense of pilgrimage and divine restlessness.

Bible reading

Genesis 12:1–9: Abraham is called to a pilgrim life.

Application

1. How do you experience the Holy Spirit in your life? Have you, like Patrick, felt the Spirit at work in or through you in your dreams? How has the Spirit changed you inside?
2. How open are you to adventure? Do you enjoy travelling? If so, what is it that you enjoy about it? Is God leading you on new adventures? What risks can you take for God? What luggage holds you down?
3. How open is your church to the Wild Goose? Does it need to let go of a desire to domesticate the Spirit in any way? What adventures do you think God is leading you to embark on as a church?

Prayer

Father, we thank you for Brendan's adventures for Christ and his drawing together of families and friends into communities of love. Kindle in us a spirit of endless adventure and a love that forges fresh bonds of community. Amen

A blessing for the journey:

Go forth with the vision of God;
Sail into the ocean of his love.
May the Sacred Three surround and sustain you
Till they bring you to your eternal home.[9]

⊕

Community

David

With the departure of the Roman soldiers early in the fifth century and the advance of Anglo-Saxon invaders into southern Britain, the Celtic peoples of Britain were pushed west and north. Many retreated to Cornwall and then travelled to the safety of Wales. While it must have been a very disturbing time, it had great benefit for the gospel, because this movement of population enabled the Christian faith to be spread with even greater speed. The Celtic fire was burning bright at Bishop Martin's monastery at Tours, and many monks travelled from there across the channel to Cornwall and then on to Wales, establishing the first monastery at Llanbelig in Snowdonia. We read earlier that the spiritual warrior Illtyd formed his monastic community at Llaniltud Fawr in Glamorgan, and it was to this great training centre that the young David came.

He was born around AD500 on the westerly tip of Pembroke-shire, which is an area of windswept heathland then known as Menevia. According to legend, his mother, St Non, gave birth to him during a thunderstorm. He was brought up in the faith, not only learning to read but also learning the book of Psalms by heart. He became a monk at Ty Gwyn under the Abbot Paulinus. On one occasion, the two went to an island together to find out how God wanted to use them. Paulinus told David that he was being called to gather 'bundles of souls' for the kingdom. Inspired by his time at Llaniltud Fawr and also at Candida Casa (Ninian's community in Scotland), David gathered a mission team and established a total of twelve monastic centres in Somerset, Lincoln, Derby, Hereford and his native Wales.

Later, David and three close friends spent time praying under the shadow of the Black Mountains and waiting on God for guidance. They were guided by God to build a large permanent mission centre in the valley where David had been born, the site of the present St David's Cathedral. This became a very remarkable community, being an educational and spiritual centre and also sending out countless mission teams to Wales and beyond. David became a bishop in 540 and died probably in 589. His final words to the people of Wales were, 'Be happy and keep your faith, and do the little things you have heard and seen me do.' It was said that after his death kings mourned him as a judge, the older people as a brother, and the younger as a father.

It was not surprising that the Celtic church was so committed to community life. There were three influences that had a bearing on this. The first was the influence of the pre-Christian society. Peter Beresford Ellis writes, 'Celtic society displayed a primitive communism, or community-ism, which by the 5th Century AD, when the Brehon Laws of Ireland were first being codified, had developed into a highly sophisticated social system.'[1]

Celtic society readily formed itself into communities of folk who had a keen interest in the needs and rights of individuals. There was in existence a primitive 'welfare state'. Under Celtic law the responsibility for providing for the sick or handicapped lay with the tribe, a responsibility that was taken very seriously. It is reckoned that Celtic society had six social classes, and a person's position in society was related to their ability and service to the community. As we have seen in Chapter 4, women were more respected in Celtic society than in any of its European contemporaries, and it was not uncommon for women to rule as chieftains. The Christian church inherited a model of community that could be very easily translated and adapted to Christianity.

The second influence was that of the Desert Fathers and Mothers, who were a great inspiration to the Celtic church. As we saw in Chapter 1, this renewal movement was fuelled by the compromise and nominalism that were affecting large parts of the church throughout the Roman Empire. Much of the life and witness of the Desert Christians was carried out in community. It was the beginning of monasticism, and a form of monasticism that the Celtic church found very attractive. Although the climate and geography of Britain were very different from the hot deserts of Egypt, the principles of simplicity, prayer, fasting, spiritual warfare, wisdom and evangelism were easy to translate to the lives of these island communities.

The third influence was the Celtic church's love for the Trinity. For them, the Father, Son and Holy Spirit were existing in perfect community, and therefore the church needed to express community life as it sought to serve the God who is Three. As Esther de Waal explains, 'The prominence given to the Trinity conveys to us something of how these men and women felt about themselves and their world. A God who is Trinity in unity challenges self-centred isolation and points instead to fellowship.'[2]

With these influences so deeply engrained, the life of the Christian church inevitably revolved around communities. Ian Bradley has written on this subject:

The dominant institution of Celtic Christianity was neither the parish church nor the cathedral, but the monastery, which sometimes began as a solitary hermit's cell and often grew to become a combination of commune, retreat house, mission station, hotel, hospital, school, university, arts centre and power-house for the local community—a source not just of spiritual energy but also of hospitality, learning and cultural enlightenment.[3]

The Celtic monastery

These communities were found scattered all over Britain and Ireland. Some of them were tiny communities of only a few huts, but others, like Columba's on Iona or Brigid's at Kildare, were huge and made quite an impact on the wider community of the nation. There were celibate and married monks. Some communities were single sex; others were mixed. It was not uncommon for women to be abbesses of mixed communities, as was the case in Hilda's community at Whitby.

Life in the monasteries varied. Some, following the example of the Desert Fathers, sought out remote and wild places and practised lives of austerity. Many of the rocks and scattered isles around the shores of these lands were occupied by hermits or small monastic communities. As previously mentioned, visitors to Skellig Michael, the rocky island off the south-west tip of the Kerry coast, can still see the ancient beehive cells that have survived centuries of Atlantic gales. Other communities were far less ascetic, although always simple.

The typical monastery would have been a gently busy place in which there was a steady rhythm of work, study, prayer and mission. Rhigyfarch, the twelfth-century biographer of David, described life in his monastery: 'They place the yoke upon their shoulders; they dig the ground tirelessly with mattocks and spades; they carry hoes and saws for cutting, and provide with their own efforts for all the needs of the community.' Ray Simpson, Guardian of The Community of Aidan and Hilda, writes of David's community:

After work in the fields, there was study before they chanted psalms in church and knelt in vigil until twilight. After a simple meal and three more hours of prayer, they slept till cockcrow. They had all things in common, no one should even say 'this is my book'. Their clothing was basic, mainly skins. David upheld St Paul's rule: 'If a person will not work, he will not eat.' Although the brothers had only one proper meal each day, they prepared appetising meals for the sick and aged guests. The 10th century Laws of Howell make clear that the monasteries were more a fellowship than a hierarchy. Though the abbot had particular responsibilities, gifts of money had to be shared equally between them all. The large monasteries were divided into households each of which had one priest.[4]

Every monastery, whether large or small, was called a *muinntir*, which means 'people'. The Celtic monasteries were very keen to emphasise the human character of these communities and were distinctly suspicious of their hierarchical institutional counterparts in Europe, which were far less personal. Each person in the communities was responsible to an *anamchara*, which means 'soul friend'. The idea of the soul friend came directly from the Desert communities. There, the soul friend would be a kind of spiritual guide and counsellor, one with whom you could share your own spiritual growth. Soul friends were a very important part of the support structure of the Celtic communities, and there was a well-known saying at the time that a person without a soul friend was like a body without a head. Soul friends had no status; they could be clergy or lay, and this system dispersed the authority of the community away from one particular person or hierarchical group to a network of support people.

All bishops would be part of a community and would respect the authority of their community. They were bishops of communities of people, rather than ruling areas of land. The idea of 'ruling a diocese' was quite foreign to the Celtic way of thinking. At the heart of the monastery was worship in the chapel, which was a building of simple construction. If they had built with stone, I feel that they would have been more inclined to follow the custom of the Eastern Orthodox churches, which have been modelled on the simplicity and beauty of a flowering plant rather than a fortress with towers and battlements.

Community and healing the land

The Celtic church flourished at a time when there was a great deal of tribal conflict among the various religious groups that made up the lands we now call Britain and Ireland. But with the spread of Christianity, the communities became resources for healing the hurts and divisions between the wider communities. The irrepressible urge in the Celtic heart to travel meant that there was much to-ing and fro-ing between communities and an eagerness to learn about how other tribes and nations worked and thought.

Pre-Christian Celts were certainly bold warriors and enjoyed conquering land, but the Christianised Celts preferred to do their warfare in the 'heavenlies' and to work for peace between nations and tribal groups. Sadly, the Anglo-Saxon invasions destroyed many of their attempts at healing the land. Different parts of the country certainly had their own identities and were proud of them, but the invasions of the Anglo-Saxons disturbed much of this feeling. For example, the Celtic peoples in the west called themselves Cymru, 'the land of comrades'. (The name Cymru was also used of the Celts in the north-west, which is why we have the name 'Cumbria' today.) However, the invading Anglo-Saxons renamed the area Wales, which means 'the land of foreigners'. This is a typical example of the suspicions, caricatures and prejudices that developed with the emergence of the separate nations of Wales, England, Scotland and Ireland, and one cannot but feel that the community that God intended for this group of islands has been regularly damaged by the darkness of evil and human sin. The respect that is now widely given to our Celtic history in these lands has done much to contribute to a healing between the nations.

As we study the Celtic church, we find a most appealing network of Christian communities that speak powerfully to our often individualistic and fragmented church today. It is encouraging to discover that there was a time in the history of these lands when genuine *koinonia* (Christian fellowship) existed and flourished, and, as we shall see in Chapter 8, this played a key role in evangelism. The Celtic church modelled a community life that was non-exclusive and deeply attractive to a confused and broken society. In this 21st century, where we see evidence of so much polarisation, not only in our world but in the church as well, more than anything else we need a church to model a Spirit-inspired community, where people demonstrate a commitment to overcoming the differences that have too easily divided us. We are seeing some encouraging examples of community-based church life in our world. For example, the now well-established Roman Catholic base communities flourishing among the poor of Latin America have a lot in common with these Celtic communities, and they have become one of the most effective evangelistic witnesses that we have today. But in Britain I feel that we still have a long way to go before we emulate the example set by our Christian forebears. We see so much individualisation and fragmentation of community around us, and therefore the need is great for churches not only to demonstrate genuine community life but also to contribute to the development of community life where we live and witness. It is encouraging to see movements like Faithworks (www.faithworks.info) becoming influential in our society. Their website states that 'Faithworks seeks to (1) Empower and inspire Christians and churches to develop their role at the hub of their community; (2) Challenge and change public perception of the Church, engaging both government and media; (3) Encourage unity and partnership.'

My feeling is that David and the other community leaders of his time would have been very much at home with this ambition, which is rooted in unity and sees the potential for community-minded groups of Christians to transform society.

Bible reading

Acts 2:41–47: The fellowship of the early church.

Application

1. One of the direct results of the coming of the Holy Spirit to the church at Pentecost was the gift of community. Take some time to reflect on your church. To what extent is it a community? How does its life compare with that of the early Celtic communities? What can you do to foster a deeper *koinonia* in your church?
2. Do you have an *anamchara*, or soul friend/spiritual director? If not, would you find it useful to have someone whom you could meet from time to time to share your spiritual journey? Is there someone you could approach who could become your soul friend?[5]

3. What kind of model of community does your church offer to the wider community around you? Does it speak of a radical alternative to the values of individualism and materialism espoused by many today?

Prayer

May the love of the Three give birth to a new community.
May the yielding of the Three give birth to a new humanity.
May the life of the Three give birth to a new creativity.
May the togetherness of the Three give birth to a new unity.
May the glory of the Three give birth to new life.[6]

Creation

Columba

In the early summer of AD521 in County Donegal, a young woman called Eithne, who was expecting her first child, had a dream. In this dream an angel came to her holding a garment that shimmered with light. He held the dazzling garment in the breeze and it seemed to float over the hills and valleys to a great distance. He said to her, 'You will have a son, and his light and influence shall be carried far—far beyond the hills you can see or the world you hear of. He will belong to God and he will bring many souls into the kingdom of God.' On 7 December that year, Columba was born, and he was indeed to travel far and bring many souls into God's kingdom.

From an early age it was clear that Columba had a special calling on his life, and as a child he was nicknamed Columcille, meaning 'Dove of the Church'. He was made a deacon at Moville, County Down, in 540, and then moved to Clonard in County Meath. Finnian had founded a monastery there in 520, which, by the time Columba arrived, numbered about 3000 students. But he was not one for settling, and he was soon on the move again. He travelled north to Ulster, where he established a monastic settlement at Derry in 546. He always had a special love for Derry, the reason being, he wrote, 'for its quietness, for its purity; for it is full of angels white, from one end to the other'. Such was his love for God's creation that he made sure the monastery was built without a tree being felled. In one of his poems he wrote that he was more afraid of the sound of an axe in Derry wood than he was of hell itself.

The Celtic restlessness was strong in Columba and he spent the next 15 years planting churches and monasteries—probably as many as 300. In 560 Columba's life was dramatically changed when he was accused of illegally copying a very precious and beautiful Book of Psalms. Columba was deeply hurt by this incident, not least by the king who opposed him. His anger burned within him to such an extent that in 561 he got involved in a major battle at Cul Dreimne against the king, a battle that the king lost. It was well known that Columba was behind the opposing forces, and a synod was called in which Columba was judged. It was clear that, as penance, he would have to leave his beloved homeland, which must have hurt him deeply, though with his travelling instinct he would have welcomed any adventure. He sought advice from his soul friend, a hermit of Lough Erme, and he was told that he must win as many souls for Christ as had been lost in the battle at Cul Dreimne.

Thus it was that Columba set off on his famous voyage in 563 with twelve companions. The wind swept his little boat across the sea to the rugged island of Iona, where he formed a monastery that soon became one of the most influential mission centres ever to exist. Visitors to Iona today are still captivated by the light, the colours of the rocks and stones, the wildness of the Atlantic waves and winds, the remoteness of the little island, and perhaps most of all by a sense of the Spirit of God, who has moved and inspired many generations of Christian people since Columba's arrival. Columba died on Iona on 9 June 597, the same year that Augustine arrived in Canterbury on his Roman mission to convert the English. Our knowledge of Columba comes from his biographer Adomnan, who describes Columba as a man 'gladdened in his inmost heart by the joy of the Holy Spirit'.

Columba was a figure who was greatly loved by the Celtic church, not least because of his love for creation. This love is beautifully expressed in one of his poems:

Delightful it is to stand on the peak of a rock, in the bosom of the isle, gazing on the face of the sea.

I hear the heaving waves chanting a tune to God in heaven; I see their glittering surf.

I see the golden beaches, their sands sparkling; I hear the joyous shrieks of the swooping gulls.

I hear the waves breaking, crashing on rocks, like thunder in heaven. I see the mighty whales.

I watch the ebb and flow of the ocean tide; it holds my secret, my mournful flight from Eire.

Contrition fills my heart as I hear the sea; it chants my sins, sins too numerous to confess.

Let me bless almighty God, whose power extends over sea and land, whose angels watch over all.

Let me study sacred books to calm my soul; I pray for peace, kneeling at heaven's gate.

Let me do my daily work, gathering seaweed, catching fish, giving food to the poor.

Let me say my daily prayers, sometimes chanting, sometimes quiet, always thinking God.

Delightful it is to live on a peaceful isle, in a quiet cell, serving the King of kings.[1]

This is a beautiful example of the Celtic church's ability to experience God in his creation. Columba starts by standing on a rock, gazing out to sea. As he hears the sound of the sea, it becomes for him a heavenly tune. The waves speak to him of the thunder of heaven. As he watches the tide ebb and flow, it speaks to him of comings and goings, and it causes him to reflect on his departure from Ireland. Here he is taken into a time of remorse and repentance as he thinks about Cul Dreimne, but he is not taken into condemnation. No, God has forgiven him and therefore he can bless the Lord, whose power extends over sea and land. He reflects further on what he sees, and he thinks about his daily work of studying, gathering food and feeding the poor. Finally, he is moved to think about prayer, which, like the sea, is sometimes still and quiet and at other times is filled with song.

The poem is a hymn of praise that has been aroused in Columba as he stands on his rock and listens to God's good creation. There is no pantheism here. His is a true and godly appreciation of nature, an appreciation that is seen in many of the psalms, which Columba would have learned by heart. The Celts loved the psalms, not least because of their love for creation. The poem above is full of the imagery of Psalm 29:

The voice of the Lord is over the waters;
the God of glory thunders,
the Lord, over mighty waters.
The voice of the Lord is powerful;
the voice of the Lord is full of majesty. (vv. 3–4, NRSV)

Such biblical passages as these appealed very much to the Celts, whose previous Druid-led pagan religion also had a very high regard for nature. Ian Finlay writes:

The Celtic church grew among people who were not builders, who were not tempted to follow a tradition of containing their gods in temples, but felt closer to them where they felt the wind buffeting their faces, and saw the flash of white wings against the sky, and smelled the sun-warmed bark of trees.[2]

The Christian community saw nothing wrong with this respect for nature and they found it very easy to incorporate it into their Christian life and witness. In fact, their Christian faith enhanced their love for creation, and many Celtic communities were formed in wild and remote places, for it was here that they could feel the power of the wind and the strength of the sea. Anyone who has been to Lindisfarne or Iona during bad weather will know all about this. The first time I visited Lindisfarne, the rain fell continuously and most of the time horizontally, carried by the north-easterly gale. I clearly remember walking round the coast of the island in these conditions, getting soaked and buffeted, and feeling so aware of the power and glory of God. How sad that we have got into the mentality of thinking that storms are something to shelter from! In our Western society, where we do all we can to protect ourselves from cold, wind and wet, we miss something of the closeness to creation that those early Celtic communities experienced. This protectiveness has been partly to blame for our lack of concern for creation and ecological issues. Furthermore, by sheltering indoors we may be missing vital parts of the Christian message. Calvin Miller, best known for his *Singer* trilogy, came to Celtic Christianity later in life after a highly significant visit to Iona, and found that it deeply refreshed his faith. He writes about the inspiration it has given to his prayer life in his book, *The Path of Celtic Prayer*.[3] In a chapter on 'Nature prayer', he writes of his admiration for the Celtic love of creation:

I believe that the Celts had this right. I have come late to this beautiful, ancient truth. I first felt its power, I believe, in the writings of Esther de Waal, which I read in 1999, but by the time I had visited Iona in 2005 I was convinced that we who serve an entirely indoor God have lost a great part of our faith. We must break through the cold, hard walls of our institutionalised worship and reach for the soft, warm reality of God that is found out of doors... Our indoor God is too small. We need to view him through the universe he created.[4]

Confining our faith to indoors also contributes to our lack of any sense of adventure. David Adam, in his book *Borderlands*, also writes about our need to encounter God out of doors, especially in those risky border places. He writes:

Today we are very much in danger of producing 'midlander' mentality and emotions: those of safe people who have never been all at sea or experienced the 'cliffs of fall' (as the poet Gerard Hopkins described the mind's mountains of grief). We avoid being frontiersmen and women in case we are shot at by our own side if we dare to cross boundaries. Borders may be hard to see or define, but we forever cross into new lands. Frontiers are still exciting places and everyone should be encouraged to explore them: the borderlands are there for us all to enjoy.[5]

If we have never spent time in natural borderlands, such as where the land meets the ocean or where day becomes night, then we will find the borderlands of human experience harder to face and understand.

God's presence in creation

Jesus frequently referred to nature when he wanted to teach an important spiritual truth. In fact, it seems that he spent a lot of time teaching the disciples how to understand the many messages in creation. Noel O'Donoghue's book *The Mountain Behind the Mountain* takes its title from a phrase in a poem by Kathleen Raine called 'The wilderness'. One stanza in this poem reads:

Yet I have glimpsed the bright mountain behind the mountain,
Knowledge under the leaves, tasted the bitter berries red,
Drunk cold water and clear from an inexhaustible hidden fountain.

O'Donoghue explains the Celtic understanding of the phrase 'the mountain behind the mountain':

The mountain of that kind of Celtic tradition to which Kathleen Raine belongs, and which nurtured the people from which I came, is neither an ideal nor a mythical mountain, nor is it exactly a holy or sacred mountain in the sense of a mountain made sacred by theophany or transfiguration. No, it is a very ordinary, very physical, very material mountain, a place of sheep and kine, of peat, and of streams that one might fish in or bathe in on a summer's day. It is an elemental mountain, of earth and air and water and fire, of sun and moon and wind and rain. What makes it special for me and for the people from which I come is that it is a place of Presence and a place of presences. Only those who can perceive this in its ordinariness can encounter the mountain behind the mountain.[6]

The Celtic church was always on the lookout for signs of God's presence in his creation. David Adam writes of how Celtic Christians sought to develop the eye of the eagle, a creature they much admired:

They prayed that their eyes might be opened, that all their senses might be made alert to that which was invisible. They prayed that they might have the eagle's eye to see Him who comes at all times... They soared to the heights of awareness and saw deeper than many peoples, for they sought to see with the eye of the eagle.[7]

The Celtic church therefore carried this expectation of meeting God in his creation, constantly on the lookout for something new to learn from him through the multitude of parables available to them. They were aware of his presence and also of the presence of his messengers, the angels. References to angels are frequent in the stories of the Celtic saints, and they treated them as a very normal part of God's creation. There are also many references to demons. Furthermore, those who have died in faith are also part of this created order. Places where people died and laid their bones in the earth were very important to the Celtic church. The burial place was a reminder of the company of witnesses who pray for us and encourage us (Hebrews 12:1), so such places were hallowed ground and good places in which to pray.

Care for creation

The Celtic love for creation included the animal world. Just as, in the wilderness, Jesus was with wild beasts who were not hostile to him, so the Celtic church recognised that people giving themselves to prayer could be less fearful of the animal kingdom. There are many stories of Celtic saints showing love and concern for animals and birds, and, indeed, many stories of animals and birds showing concern for the saints.

Cuthbert seems to have had a special affection for the animal kingdom. There is a famous story about Cuthbert when he was prior at Melrose and had been invited by Abbess Aebbe to spend a few days at the mixed convent at Coldingham. It was apparently his custom at night to go into the sea up to his shoulders and pray for hours at a stretch in the cold waters. This in itself tells us something about the effect of prayer in relation to creation. The story we have of Cuthbert is that at the end of one night vigil in the water, he came to the shore, whereupon two otters bounded out of the water and warmed his feet with their breath and tried to dry him with their fur. Later in his life, when he was on Farne Island, there is a story of him speaking sternly to the crows who were eating all the seeds he was sowing. 'Why are you eating crops you yourselves did not grow?' he asked them indignantly. 'Perhaps you have greater need of them than I. If God has given you permission, then do as He bade you; if not, be off with you and stop damaging other people's property!' Apparently they duly obeyed. Bede, telling us this story, informs us that Cuthbert was inspired by the Desert Father Anthony, who spoke severely to a donkey that was threatening to trample down his little garden.[8]

Columbanus was said to be very fond of a number of wild beasts who would come and play with him. On one occasion, twelve wolves came up to him while he was saying a psalm. So taken were they by Columbanus and the psalm that they meekly stood by him before going away. There are also stories of his talking to the squirrels. Such stories of Cuthbert and Columbanus should not be seen simply as quaint, because they carry a much deeper significance. It is not at all unlikely that the very strong presence of the Spirit of God in such people affected the animals' response to them. In Romans 8:19–24, Paul tells us of the eager yearning in creation to be freed from its bondage to decay and its waiting for the revelation of the children of God. According to this passage, the Spirit has a key role in this releasing. Certainly it was the expectation of the Celtic church that the outpouring of the Spirit on God's people would influence creation. This theme was taken up delightfully by Francis, whose love for creation was so much at the heart of his spirituality. It is interesting to note that Columbanus established a community at Bobbio in Italy, to which the young Francis came in later years. He was greatly impressed by this Celtic community and it was here that he developed his love for creation. There is therefore at Bobbio a historical connection between Celtic and Franciscan spirituality.

We have, then, in the Celtic church a thoroughly creation-affirming spirituality. But this creation-centredness was not at the cost of redemption. Because they were so attuned to it, Celtic Christians became very much aware of creation's signals about the need for the redeeming work of Christ. A Celtic saint who illustrates this well is Chad, who formed a monastic community at Lichfield. Bede tells us that 'if a gale rose while he was reading or doing anything else he would at once call upon God for mercy and pray him to show mercy on mankind'. The stronger the storm, the more earnest was Chad's praying. When his monks asked Chad why he did this, he replied, 'Have you not read, "The Lord thundered in the heavens, and the Highest gave his voice"?' He was quick to point out that the thunder and lightning were intended to remind people of the judgment to come, and our response should be to 'examine our inmost hearts, purging the vileness of our sins'.[9] The Celtic church was all too aware of the damage done to creation by human sin and Satan's rebellion, and thus they had a great love for the cross. You can still see today, in Ireland, many examples of huge standing crosses, planted firmly in the soil as a sign of Christ's redeeming work in the heart of God's good, but damaged, creation. In the words of Euros Bowen, a modern Welsh poet, '*Nid oes atgyfodiad lle nad oes pridd*' ('There is no resurrection where there is no earth').[10]

As we saw in Chapter 3, the Celtic Christians were also very aware of evil influences in creation and felt a keen sense of responsibility to cleanse the earth where it had been spoilt or infected in some way. Generally speaking, the church in the West since those Celtic times has been rather indifferent to creation, so now, when we are facing an ecological crisis, it is disappointing but not surprising to discover that the church is not at the forefront of caring for our planet.

Noel O'Donoghue talks about the *priestly* role of the church in bringing together the divine and human worlds. God has ordained it that the Christian community is empowered to have a great influence for good on this earth. We have been entrusted with the work of blessing our land, but if we fail to do this, there are principalities and powers of darkness that are all too ready to contaminate the earth. Our failure to take this priestly duty seriously has allowed much darkness to spread in our lands. Old customs like beating the bounds and rogation days developed from a spirituality that saw the sense in blessing the ground. Today we are seeing such customs being restored as spiritually effective rituals that bless the earth on which we live. I am sure we shall see other rituals developing as we take this priestly role more seriously.

The creation-centred strand of the Celtic woven cord is probably the one that has proved to be the most popular in recent years, and it is very encouraging to see how this spirituality is driving us back outdoors again, to listen to and love the creation that God has entrusted to our care, and to use its rich imagery in our worship. We have some catching up to do, and there's a way to go, but at least we are on the road.

Bible reading

Genesis 1:1—2:3: God made the good earth.

Application

1. What do you feel about creation? Have you experienced hearing God though his creation? What can you do to become more aware of God speaking to you in this way?
2. Have you been in a natural 'borderlands' place? How did it feel? Why not plan to go for a walk in the rain?
3. Is there any way in which you can show your concern for creation? How can you fulfil your 'priestly duty' to the creation around your home? Is there land around you that needs healing, either because it is physically polluted by chemicals and waste, for example, or because it is spiritually polluted by a history of battles or human sin and injustice? Is there any action you or your church could do to bring healing to the land?

Prayer

A midday prayer:

As the press of work ceases at noon
May God's Rest be upon us.

As the sun rides high at noon
May the Sun of Righteousness shine upon us.

As the rain refreshes the stained, stale land
May the Spirit bring rain upon our dry ground.[11]

⊕

Evangelism

Columbanus

Columbanus was born in Leinster, Ireland, in AD540. As a young man he joined Comgall's monastery at Bangor, County Down, having heard the call to be a monk through a woman hermit. He was ordained in 572. Here he developed a reputation for being a fine scholar, but within him was the urge to take the gospel overseas. Finally, when he was over 50 years old, in 591, he felt a clear call to carry the gospel to Gaul. There he discovered a number of Celtic settlements of British people who had fled the Anglo-Saxon invasions. He moved to Burgundy and settled in a narrow valley in the foothills of the Vosges, near the Swiss–German border, where he founded a monastic community. He built his first church on the site of the ruined temple of Diana, following the Celtic custom of redeeming land once devoted to pagan worship. From here he went on to establish another community in a discarded Roman fort at Luxeuil. Here, as at Vosges, he and the community transformed a wild, barren land into a land of fruit orchards and cornfields.

Columbanus might well have settled there had he not fallen foul of the king of Burgundy, who took exception to the fact that Columbanus severely rebuked him for a wayward life that involved various mistresses and illegitimate children. The king ordered Columbanus to return to Ireland, but when he boarded the ship on the Loire, a great tidal wave came up from the estuary. The sailors were terrified and refused to take him anywhere. Columbanus simply took this as a sign that he was not to return to Ireland, so at the age of 70 he began his wanderings again, travelling this time to Switzerland, where he settled for a time by Lake Constance. He immediately began evangelising and sought to cleanse the area spiritually by chopping down sacred trees that had become idols of the occult. This aroused violent opposition from the locals, who forced Columbanus and his companions to flee over the Alps. After a short stay in Milan, they eventually settled in Bobbio, Italy, where they built a monastery. Here Columbanus died on 23 November 615.

The story of Columbanus reveals many typical aspects of Celtic (particularly Irish Celtic) ways of mission, which were spontaneous, community-based, prayerful and fearless. Columbanus was, on the whole, more ascetic and more confrontational than some of the British Celtic missionaries, but they all shared the same passionate desire to evangelise the lost. What, then, were the keys to the success of the Celtic mission? I would suggest a number of factors.

Evangelism and cultural sensitivity

First, there was a deep sensitivity about the way in which the Celtic church went about its mission. Nowhere do we get the impression of a powerful ecclesiastical force moving in on reluctant individuals. Because they were not infected by the rather depressing doctrines of the loathsomeness of humanity that were starting to emanate from some parts of Europe, they held a much more optimistic view of human beings, who were, after all, made in the image of God. While the Celtic Christians were very clear about the reality and consequences of human sin, and were not reticent in teaching about hell, they nonetheless seemed to have had a reasonably positive view of human nature, just as they had a positive view about God's good creation. For them, the two were very closely connected. God's created order was damaged but not totally sick. This meant that individuals, the land they lived on, the communities that they were part of and the way they lived were to be respected.

There are many examples of this attitude of respect. Bede tells us about Chad, that 'he travelled on foot and not on horseback when he went to preach the Gospel, whether in towns or country, in cottages, villages or strongholds; for he was one of Aidan's disciples and always sought to instruct his people by the same methods as Aidan and his own brother, Cedd'.[1] Aidan's influence of gentleness seems to have been far-reaching, which is in contrast to many forms of mission that have been used in this country, and taken to other countries subsequently. Ian Bradley writes:

The way that they worked was very different from the approach of later Christian missionaries who joined forces with traders and imperial adventurers and sought to impose their own Western values and secure a cultural as well as a religious conversion of the natives... The approach of the Celtic missionaries was essentially gentle and sensitive. They sought to live alongside the people with whom they wanted to share the good news of Christ, to understand and respect their beliefs and not to dominate or culturally condition them. [2]

All this was very different from the presentations of the gospel that had come with the Roman Christian legionaries, whose influence in this country was minimal. 'This time it was not grand governors riding in elegant chariots who carried the gospel,' writes Robert Van de Weyer, 'but barefoot monks plodding the muddy lanes.' [3]

A fine example was set by Cuthbert. When Boisil died, Cuthbert became prior of the monastery at Melrose, and we are told by Bede that Cuthbert carried out his office 'with holy zeal'. He spent part of his time in the monastery, carrying out his ministry of teaching and prayer, but often he would follow the example of Boisil and venture out from the community on evangelistic expeditions. In his travels, it seems, he encountered many people who had strayed from the faith into all kinds of superstitions, which Bede graphically describes as 'diabolical rubbish'! Cuthbert's way of evangelising was to travel to a village, sometimes on horseback but usually on foot, and, on arrival, to begin preaching. The church very quickly made an impact on the people of Northumbria. By Cuthbert's time, villagers would recognise a Christian preacher and would gather around to listen. Bede tells us of Cuthbert, 'Such was his skill in teaching, such his power of driving his lessons home, and so gloriously did his angelic countenance shine forth, that none dared keep back from him even the closest secrets of the heart.'[4] But Cuthbert did not go just to the established village communities. He went up into the hills, where other preachers dreaded going: here were small groups of the very poor, whom most tried to avoid because of their squalor. Cuthbert would quite often disappear into the hills to live among these folk, sometimes for up to a month, before returning to Melrose.

Cuthbert continued this evangelistic ministry after his spell on Farne Island as a hermit, and he used the opportunity of his ministry as a bishop once again to travel far and wide, as he had done earlier at Melrose, preaching the gospel and healing the sick. For him, as for all Celtic bishops, his ministry was not simply to the church but was a missionary ministry, which he fulfilled with great devotion until his death in 687.

Very important to Celtic mission was the spiritual gift of discernment (1 Corinthians 12:10). Because they invested so much in a prayerful opening up of their intuition and imagination to the influence of the Holy Spirit, Celtic Christians were very sensitive to presences of good and evil in people and places. They therefore sensed what was good in a community and blessed it accordingly; or they sensed evil, in which case they sought to combat it with prayer. On some occasions, especially with Columba and Patrick, we find that these combats gained almost Mount Carmel-like proportions as, in the spirit of Elijah, they challenged the occultic powers of particularly dark druids. In the main, though, this kind of contest was not common and much of what they found in the communities they ministered to were things they could either bless or Christianise.

Thus, for example, when they began to evangelise Derbyshire, my home county, they discovered a village custom of worshipping water divinities at the rivers and wells. Various divinities were honoured at these water places. When the Christians came, they did not attack the customs by performing dazzling exorcisms and engaging in glorious victories over the enemy, as would happen in some charismatic circles today, where any whiff of the demonic is attacked with great gusto. Such engagement can often arise from our own need for power rather than the presence of spiritual conflict, and the Celtic communities were deeply suspicious of Christian power-games. Rather, they would listen carefully to the community's desire to give thanks for the gift of water, and they would bless their need to give thanks for and honour the gift, while at the same time proclaiming the cross of Christ over the place and making clear the need for redemption. I am sure that in some cases this would have involved some kind of exorcistic ministry, with fasting and prayer, where they discerned that the site had been spoilt in any way by dark powers.

So, in Derbyshire we find that a number of wells had their names changed, often with such sensitivity that the names stayed almost the same. For example, a well dedicated to the water sprite Eilan was rededicated to St Helen. The Celtic church also encouraged the custom of annual thanksgiving for water, and they converted the pagan well-dressing ceremonies into Christian celebrations. You can go round Derbyshire towns and villages in the summer and come across many such celebrations, and many of the themes of the beautiful floral pictures are still based on Bible stories.

All this feels very risky, for surely, you would think, there is a real danger of syncretism. But the Celtic church did not fear this because it was so deeply rooted in the word of God and knew such a vibrancy in the power of the Spirit. They had great confidence that their love for Jesus and his word would prevent them from straying into forbidden territories. They had great confidence that the Holy Spirit would give them the discernment that would alert them to any tendency to return to evil. Where necessary, they did engage in confrontational measures, as in the case of Columbanus in Switzerland, when he destroyed the occultic trees. Perhaps, in this case, the trees had been carved and used in such a way that it was impossible to restore them to their original condition. But generally the Celtic Christians sought to redeem and reform. They had much more confidence in the word and the Spirit than do those charismatic evangelicals today who are very fearful of any attempt to understand modern forms of paganism. We can learn much from the Celtic church's confidence here, a confidence that enabled it to listen rather than dominate, and a confidence that could discern when to Christianise sensitively and when to confront dark powers.

I see something of a parallel with this in some of the Fresh Expressions that are emerging in the church today. Not far from where I live, Mark, a Pioneer Minister who has been a heavy metal musician for some years, is church planting into the heavy metal music culture. Some years ago, evangelical Christians would have held up their hands in horror at the thought of Christians listening to such music, let alone encouraging worship in that style! However, times are changing, and now Mark is blessed by the bishop and encouraged by the evangelical churches in the team where he serves to develop this Fresh Expression of church. I believe that such expressions of mission are very much in keeping with the way our Celtic forebears took the gospel to those who had no knowledge of Christ. It combines a respect for other people's culture with an ability to learn and speak their language, while at the same time being clear about the claims of the gospel and listening out for any influences of darkness that have used that particular culture to oppress people.

Evangelism and power

This leads to the second important feature of Celtic evangelism, which is to do with their understanding of power. We shall look at this aspect more fully in Chapter 15, but it needs to be mentioned here because it was an important feature of Celtic evangelism. Many of the stories of the miraculous were in the context of mission, and the Celtic church would have been quite at home with a phrase that was common parlance in charismatic circles in the 1980s—'Power Evangelism'. It came from a movement led by John Wimber that sought to get charismatic healing out of the church to become part of evangelistic witness. Today we are seeing the emergence of a movement generally known as 'Healing on the Streets'. Originating in Belfast, this movement has inspired many churches literally to take healing on to the streets. On Saturday morning, small groups from the church set up shop on the high street and offer healing to passers-by. A website that I checked out at the time of writing invited people to a conference on this subject by encouraging them to imagine:

Imagine your own region alive to the glory of God, encountering him through his people and awakened to his reality among them. Imagine healing, signs and wonders OUT THERE among the people as you impact your community with Kingdom power and authority. If you can imagine this… then you are ready to discover just what happens when the church leaves the building.[5]

I can imagine the early Celtic church reading that and saying, 'Well, where else would you expect to find it?' They were an extraordinarily 'out there' kind of church and their expectation was that when you went out there, the power of God went with you to change lives through signs and wonders. The Celtic peoples of the time would have had no difficulty with the concept of supernatural power; their concerns would be to do with where it came from and why it was being used.

In the stories of Celtic mission, it is clear that the power of the Spirit is closely linked with personal holiness and with remarkable humility. No doubt these believers felt a strong affinity with Paul, who wrote to the Corinthian church, 'And I came to you in weakness and in fear and in much trembling. My speech and my proclamation were not with plausible words of wisdom, but with a demonstration of the Spirit and of power' (1 Corinthians 2:3–4). By its humility and authenticity, the church showed that it was not interested in using this power for dominance, but genuinely wanted to demonstrate that the love of God could break in powerfully on people's lives to rescue, heal and deliver them.

Their witness challenges the unbelief in the church today, which is only just beginning to emerge from the cold grip of rationalism. It also challenges the tendency of many charismatic churches who have discovered the power of God but keep it confined to the church in healing services and conferences. And it also challenges those who practise a healing and deliverance ministry at evangelistic meetings, but do it in a style too closely connected with the ways of human power, where the extravert evangelist with loud voice and garish suit, backed up by an imposing platform party, communicates a message that has more to do with manipulation than with the demonstration of the power of God through human weakness.

Evangelism and community

A third feature of the Celtic church's evangelism was its community base, which we have already discussed in Chapter 6. The monastic communities were not only places to which interested people could come and learn about the faith, but they also became schools and universities, hospitals and centres for social care of all kinds, thus drawing in large numbers of non-Christian people who encountered a community with a living faith in God. Furthermore, these communities acted as mission stations, which trained men and women in preaching and healing and sent them out on missions. Many of those who went out from the communities did not return, for they formed other communities made up of newly converted people. Sometimes individuals would go out on their own to live a hermit life, but, as happened in the deserts of Egypt, others would come and gather near their hut or cave and a small community would develop. The church grew so fast because these cells were so wonderfully flexible and unrestrained by any institution that they could easily multiply.

Some, like Chad's brother Cedd, seemed to be called to a particular ministry in church and monastery planting. Consecrated as Bishop of the East Saxons, Cedd set up a number of churches and communities in his evangelistic work among these people. Bede records, 'To the great joy of the king and all the people, the Gospel of eternal life made daily headway throughout the province for a considerable time.'[6] There is no doubt that the network of evangelistic communities had an immense impact.

One of the reasons why the community base was so important is that it provided great security in a society that was deeply troubled and constantly under threat. With Roman civilisation collapsing, which had been so secure for so long, and the new civilisations of the Angles, Saxons and Jutes pushing in from the east, it was a time of massive cultural change, and the little Christian communities provided oases of security. There are parallels with Western society today. With the prevailing culture of the Enlightenment era disintegrating, and with all kinds of new influences coming in from many different directions, there are increasing signs of profound anxiety in our society. In addition, the hitherto strong nuclear community unit of the family is under great threat. Furthermore, our attempts at wider unity, such as in the European Community, seem constantly to flounder. But God has put it into the heart of all people to belong to community, for we are made in his image and he is in the community of the Holy Trinity. Essential to our proclamation of the good news, therefore, is that we proclaim a community based not on values of ideology, consumerism or rationalism, but rather on the counter-culture of the Sermon on the Mount.

Probably the most successful tool of the current era is Alpha, and it is often said that a strong feature of this course is the shared meal. A meal is a fundamental part of community, and the early Celtic evangelists would have very much affirmed this rooting of evangelistic preaching in hospitality and community. Those who come to faith do so in the context of community, and that is a great strength of the course. Once again, we see that the values running deep in that early Celtic church have great relevance for our mission today.

Evangelism and abandonment

The fourth feature of Celtic evangelism that we need to notice today is its wonderful sense of joyful abandonment. Few Celtic missions were formally planned. It was much more a case of setting off from the community, asking God to direct their steps, and being open to his surprises. Spontaneity was the order of the day. Aidan's way of evangelising was typical:

Whether in town or country, he always travelled on foot unless compelled by necessity to ride; and whatever people he met on his walks, whether high or low, he stopped and spoke to them. If they were heathen he urged them to be baptised; and if they were Christians he strengthened their faith.[7]

People like Aidan would return in due course to their community, but others, like Columbanus, were willing to venture out even to far-off lands, not knowing where they would end up. As we have seen, these people were called *peregrinati*, perpetual wanderers.

The fundamental difference between the early Celtic church and much of the church today is that the Celtic church was utterly given to mission. It thought, lived and breathed mission. It could understand no Christianity that did not include mission. It had no interest in bureaucracies and institutions that existed simply to support the church. It had a wild, childlike, simple and overwhelming passion to see men, women and children of its own land and beyond find faith in Jesus Christ, and gave itself utterly to that end. If nothing else compels us to respect the Celtic church, this feature of its life should do so. In our spiritual roots of Christian faith in Britain, we find a sensitive, powerful, community-based, carefree missionary church. Perhaps this church, more than any other, discovered what God has truly given to these islands— a missionary responsibility that is not to do with the imposition of Western culture and manipulation but with a humble, foolish abandonment to the gospel of the Lord Jesus, who died, was raised and sits at the right hand of God.

Bible reading

1 Corinthians 2:1–5: The gospel, human weakness and the power of God.

Application

1. How sensitive is the evangelism of your church? What parts of the culture around your church are you able to bless? What parts need to be challenged? How can you go about affirming the good and challenging the bad? Are there aspects of life in your community that you could Christianise in some way?
2. How much of a community is your local church? How evangelistically effective is the community life of your church? Is the quality of life in your church community better than in the secular community around you? If so, what are the differences? If not, why not?
3. In what way can you be like the *peregrinati*? Why not try wandering out into the neighbourhood to see whom God causes you to meet? Can you think of ways in which your church can engage more in this 'carefree evangelism'? How about healing in the streets?

Prayer

Kindle in our hearts, O God,
the flame of that love which never ceases,
that it may burn in us giving light to others.
May we shine for ever in your holy temple,
set on fire with your eternal light,
even your Son Jesus Christ,
our Saviour and Redeemer.[8]

PRAYER OF ST COLUMBA

⊕

Prophecy

Fursey

Fursey (sometimes called Fursa) was born in Ireland towards the end of the sixth century. Tradition has it that he was baptised by the great St Brendan. As a child, he loved reading the scriptures and he was sent to study under Abbot Meldan on the isle of Insequin in Lough Corrib, where the ruin known as Killursa (Cill Fursa) still stands today. It was not long before Fursey was involved in a very active travelling ministry, and large crowds gathered to hear him. It is clear that Fursey grew increasingly anxious about these crowds, and he retreated to a small island off the west coast of Ireland to seek God's guidance. It was here that he felt God preparing him for a new mission. Whether he knew that the king of the Angles was asking for missionaries, we do not know. But we do know that he set sail in a coracle with his two brothers and a couple of friends, either planning to travel to East Anglia or, in Celtic fashion, simply setting sail and entrusting their journey to the wind of the Spirit.

Fursey and his companions arrived on the east coast of England in AD633 to embark on their mission to the Angles. They were welcomed by King Sigebert, who had become a Christian in France. Sigebert gave Fursey a base at Burgh Castle, the site of the last fort the Romans had built before leaving Britain. Fursey spent many years there, often crossing the estuary near Great Yarmouth to bring the gospel to the people of the area we now call Norfolk. Bede tells us that 'inspired by the example of his goodness and the effectiveness of his teaching, many unbelievers were converted to

Christ, and many who already believed were drawn to greater love and faith in him'.

During this time, Fursey became very ill and, over a period of days during his illness, he experienced a series of extraordinary visions. Bede tells us that he 'quitted his body' from sunset to cockcrow, which presumably means that he was having the kind of experience Paul describes in 2 Corinthians 12. During these times he saw huge choirs of angels. He told others later that he regularly saw the souls of the departed, singing, 'The saints shall go from strength to strength' and 'The God of gods shall be seen in Sion.' But he also saw terrible visions of evil spirits, who taunted him.

On one occasion during these days of illness and visions, he was taken by some angels high up into the sky. The angels told him to look down at the earth. As he looked down, he saw a gloomy valley and four fires in the air. The angels told him that these fires were terrible desires that threatened to consume the world. The fires were: Falsehood, when Satan is not renounced and evil is pursued; Covetousness, when worldly wealth is put before the love of God; Discord, when relationships are hurt and broken; and Cruelty, when the weak are robbed and defrauded. Fursey watched these fires with horror as they grew together into one terrible conflagration, and he saw great battles between warrior angels and dark demons. At one point, Fursey was burnt by the fires in this vision, which left physical scars on his shoulder and jaw for the rest of his life. He recovered from his illness, and the rest of his life and ministry were deeply affected by his prophetic vision. So impressed by it was he that, when he related the story, we are told that he would sweat profusely, even on a bitter winter's day.

❧

The kind of prophetic vision that Fursey received was not un-common in the Celtic church. They were constantly expectant that God would show them heavenly insights that would affect their life and ministry on earth. Fursey's vision, in fact, has a remarkably pertinent message for our world today. As we survey the spiritual health of Britain, we still see evidence of those four fires: people tamper with occultism and witchcraft, and Satanism spreads; we see the fire of materialism and consumerism destroying many lives; we see a deep crisis over human relationships; and we see serious injuries to the poor and the weak. If Fursey were to be taken above Britain today, I fear he would see the same fires burning. The problem for us is that, after 200 years of Enlightenment thinking, church and secular society have lost their ability to be open to the visionary. However, there are signs that this is changing.

The Celtic church, unencumbered with the burdens of rational-ism, gave a high value to the imagination. One of the main reasons for this is that the believers were closely in touch with creation. For them, this presented them with no paradox. The material and spiritual were not to be harshly divided. Richard Harries, when he was Bishop of Oxford, wrote in his much-acclaimed book, *Art and the Beauty of God*:

One of the strengths of the Christian faith is the way it can hold together in one vision the physical and the spiritual. The world has been created good/beautiful by God. Christ has claimed it as his own and will raise it to eternal light and life. This means that the material and the immaterial, the visible and the invisible, the physical and the spiritual interpenetrate one another.[1]

Seeing and perceiving

In David Adam's *Eye of the Eagle*, he tells us of the Celtic church's love for John's Gospel, the traditional symbol of which is the eagle. The eagle was much admired by the Celtic church because it could fly higher than any other bird and it had the sharpest eyesight. They, too, longed for the ability to 'fly high' and to have sharp eyesight to see the things of God. But their seeing was not just in the kind of dramatic vision that Fursey had. The training ground for such visions was learning to see and hear God through his creation here on earth.

Jesus often communicated with his disciples through parables. He took events or ideas from this world and pointed out how they conveyed a deeper truth. In Matthew's Gospel (13:1–17), when the disciples ask Jesus why he communicates through parables, Jesus replies by quoting from the sixth chapter of Isaiah, in which the prophet describes his wonderful vision. Here Jesus connects parable-telling with vision-giving. He quotes God's words to Isaiah, in which God explains that the people to whom Isaiah will prophesy have a serious problem—seeing but not perceiving, hearing but not understanding. In other words, their hearing and seeing only go so far. Isaiah's hearing and seeing have reached a much deeper level—indeed, as far as heaven itself. The Celtic church, therefore, had a clear grasp of the parable principle.

When my children were small, they (and I!) enjoyed looking at books of stereograms. A stereogram is a picture that appears to be two-dimensional but, if you focus on it correctly, amazingly a delightful three-dimensional picture appears. You can see and then perceive a deeper, fuller picture. Dan Dychman, a pioneer in this field, explains, 'The idea of stereoviewing these images is that you will be looking *through* the images... You don't want to look directly *at the surface* of the page, but rather to gaze *through the page*.'[2] This is exactly what the Celtic church was doing as it looked at all that was painted on the pages of creation. They had learned to look through the page with their open imagination, and it is no wonder that, as a result, they were given Isaiah-type visions.

As we study the Celtic church, we find a people who were intuitively very aware, not only seeing and perceiving but also hearing all kinds of signals from heaven. Cuthbert very clearly had this imaginative ability to see with the eye of the eagle. A reading of Bede's *Life of Cuthbert* introduces us to a man whose ministry was steeped in prophetic visionary activity. As a child, he was prophesied to by an infant, and that very act seems to have indicated that prophecy was to play an important part in his ministry. His much-loved prior, Boisil, prophesied to him as they unfolded the Gospel of John, the eagle, together. Boisil was given the eagle eye into Cuthbert's life.

Bede writes of Cuthbert, not long after Boisil's death, 'Meanwhile the man of God began to grow strong in prophecy, foretelling the future and revealing to those near him events that were happening elsewhere.'[3] After Cuthbert's ten years on Farne Island, this ability seems to have been all the sharper. While on Farne Island, he was in touch with Hilda's successor, Aelfflaed, who was the sister of King Ecgfrith.[4] She had a deep affection for Cuthbert, and on one occasion when she fell sick she longed for him to come and pray for her. Not long after Aelfflaed had expressed this wish, some-one arrived with a linen cincture sent by Cuthbert. The cincture, blessed by Cuthbert, became the means of God's healing for Aelfflaed, for after two days of wearing it she was up and well. The reason Cuthbert had sent this gift was because 'her wishes had been made known to him by heavenly means'. In charismatic circles nowadays, it would be said that Cuthbert had been given a 'word of knowledge'.

Some time after this, Aelfflaed became very concerned about her brother, who, though he was a Christian, was beginning to become more aggressive in his desire to seek further land for the Northumbrians. She pleaded with Cuthbert for a meeting. Cuthbert agreed to meet her at the monastery on Coquet Island, a half-way point between Whitby and Farne Island. When they met, she begged him to tell her what was going to become of her brother. 'I know you can tell me,' she said, 'for the spirit of prophecy is strong in you.' Cuthbert was reluctant to give her a straight answer, but he clearly knew that the king would be dead within a year, and he intimated this to her. Cuthbert also had knowledge of who would succeed the king: this was Aldfrith, who was currently on the island of Iona.

That autumn, Cuthbert was persuaded by King Ecgfrith to leave his beloved Farne Island and become the Bishop of Lindisfarne. He was consecrated at York on Easter Day, 26 March 685. But Ecgfrith was on the war-path again and was pushing north into Scotland. During those forays north, Cuthbert went to Carlisle on his first episcopal visitation. The queen was there, awaiting the outcome of a fierce battle that her husband was engaged in at Nechtansmere. Cuthbert knew that his prophecy to Aelfflaed was nearing fulfilment. On the Saturday afternoon, 20 May 685, Cuthbert and the queen were being taken round the city wall to see a remarkable Roman fountain that had been built into it. Cuthbert suddenly felt very disturbed in his spirit and he partly collapsed, leaning against the wall. With a deep sigh he said, 'Perhaps at this moment the battle is being decided.' A priest nearby, panicking a little, blurted out, 'But how do you know this?' Cuthbert's answer is very interesting. He replied, 'Do you not see how strangely disturbed the air is?' It seems that Cuthbert's eagle eye had become so clear that he could sense this national disturbance in the very air around him. He had learned to look through the air, not just at it.

On the Monday, a fugitive from the battle arrived and reported that, at the very moment that Cuthbert had felt the air disturbed, the king and his bodyguards had been slaughtered in battle. Cuthbert was perhaps peculiarly gifted with a very acute prophetic sense, and no doubt Farne Island had provided an ideal training ground for this gift.

Dreams, the intuitive and guidance

One very respected medium for God's communication was that of dreams. As we saw in Chapter 4, it was a dream experienced by

Hilda's mother that revealed the extent of Hilda's future ministry. Patrick had a number of dreams that profoundly affected him. Noel Dermot O'Donoghue writes: 'There were two sources of light in the world of Patrick, son of Calpornius... Holy Scripture and his own dreams.'[5] Patrick's *Confession* is a short work but it contains seven distinct dream narratives. It was a dream that caused him to escape from Ireland, and it was another dream that caused him to return. It was in a dream that he engaged in a terrible moment of spiritual battle with Satan and it was also in a dream that he, in some mystical way, saw the Holy Spirit praying within him. Patrick was bold in speaking about his prophetic dreams because he knew that these dreams gave his ministry authority, such was the respect in which dreams were held by the Celtic church. In the secular world, there is a fast-growing interest in dream activity, but the church has been slow to catch up. Perhaps we will learn to respect our dreams again, acknowledging them as authentic God-given prophetic gifts.

This openness to the intuitive, together with the confident anticipation that God delighted to communicate with his people, meant that the Celtic church often went about its decision-making processes in rather different ways from the church of today. The latter is far more at ease with working parties and committees than it is with the dangerous world of the prophetic, which is deemed to be far too subjective and unreliable. In fact, the Celtic church was somewhat in contrast to the Roman church, which was much more at ease with models of decision-making taken from the structures of the Roman Empire. The coming of Augustine to Canterbury is an excellent example of the contrasting methods of the two churches.

In AD597, Augustine and 40 monks arrived at Canterbury to begin the Rome-initiated mission to the English. The mission was successful but, after a while, it became clear that the Roman church was significantly different from the British Celtic church. In 603, Augustine summoned some bishops to a meeting in Gloucestershire. A rather cool meeting took place, and Augustine challenged the Celtic bishops to a kind of contest to discover which church was to become the dominant church in Britain. He found a blind Englishman and asserted that whoever could heal the man would 'be followed by all'. The British priest and bishops could not heal him, but Augustine was successful. This kind of charismatic contest would have been an anathema to the Celtic church. They did, on occasions, when provoked, accept such a challenge from the pagan druids, but to engage in such a contest between Christians would be totally against their values, which rejected any sense of competitiveness.

The Celtic leaders were therefore very uneasy with this way of discerning God's will, and they asked for a further meeting. The Celts chose some bishops and leaders, mostly from the lively community at Bangor. Then they went to a hermit and asked him if they should abandon their own traditions at Augustine's command. It is very interesting to observe that they put more faith in this humble hermit than they did in the Pope's bishop to the English. Such was their confidence in the hermit's prophetic gifting that they dared ask him such a straight question. Had he said yes, it would have meant a massive upheaval for the British church. However, his reply was neither yes nor no. Bede records that he answered, 'If he [Augustine] is a man of God, follow him.' Understandably, the bishops asked how they could know this. The hermit replied that the clue would be in Augustine's humility. He said, 'If he rises courteously as you approach, rest assured that he is the servant of Christ and do as he asks. But if he ignores you and does not rise, then, since you are in the majority, do not comply with his demands.' This, then, would be the clue.

The British leaders went to meet Augustine, ready to see the signal that the hermit had alerted them to. Sadly, far from showing any humility, Augustine sat firmly in his chair and, in a fairly con-frontational way, set out to put the Celtic bishops in their place. But the bishops were not to be moved. Their hermit had spoken prophetically and, as far as they were concerned, Augustine had proved that he was not worthy to be Archbishop of Canterbury, so they could not respect him as such.[6] We may judge the Celtic leaders as simplistic, and it is certainly unfortunate that a healthier relationship with Augustine could not have been established, but the point is that they had learned to respect deeply the ministry of the hermit who, on their behalf, had devoted years to listening to God. They were not interested in charismatic competitions of power. Neither were they impressed by fine oratory, which Wilfrid was later to use at the Synod of Whitby. For them, the all-important thing was humility, and, for all the strengths of the Augustinian mission, which were many, it seems it did not have the kind of meekness that was such an inspiring feature of the Celtic church. As the Celtic church declined in these lands, so that wonderful openness to the prophetic gifts of the Spirit of God was largely lost. The Celtic church challenges us to a deeper listening to God, acknowledging that he communicates to us in a rich variety of ways. We will need to give time to making space in our busy lives to hear his voice and, when we do hear, to follow the example of meekness that characterised the prophetic ministry that was so alive in the Celtic church.

Bible reading

Isaiah 6:1–10: Isaiah is given vision to see behind the curtain, to behold the things of heaven.

Application

1. How do you listen to God? Have you ever had a vision? Think of ways of developing the ability to see and perceive, to hear and understand.

2. Do you record your dreams? Do you feel that there have been times when God has spoken to you in a dream? Ask him to open your dream life to his Spirit, that he may communicate with you in this way.

3. How does your church make decisions? Is there an openness to prophetic insight? Is prophecy encouraged in your church?

Prayer

From all that is false and flirts with evil:
Good Lord deliver us

From the love of riches and from greed and envy:
Good Lord deliver us

From insensitive words and from discord and strife:
Good Lord deliver us

From manipulation and from abuse of others:
Good Lord deliver us

Watching and praying, we draw near to you, High King of the Universe. We glimpse your awesome Presence in the gleaming pools, in the gentle coves, in storm and thunder, and in the stillness of the night. Reveal to us the mysteries of heaven; rebuke us for our wretched ways, and bring us to the place of holiness. Amen.[7]

Authenticity

Aidan

As the fifth century drew to a close, Britain found itself in a constant round of battles between the Celts and the Anglo-Saxons. The Roman armies withdrew, leaving the locals to battle it out themselves. By the end of the sixth century, the Anglo-Saxons were in control of the Midlands and the south-east, with the Celts being pushed west and north. A Celtic hero at this time was the legendary King Arthur, whose name is linked with a great victory over the Anglo-Saxons in AD516, but this victory was only temporary. The Anglo-Saxons were here to stay and, in time, the nation came to be named after the Angles: England.

It was around this time that the Pope in Rome sent his mission, led by Augustine, to evangelise the invading tribes gathered in the south-east of Britain. The missionaries made their base in Canterbury and, once settled, were joined by others to assist them. One of the newcomers was a bishop by the name of Paulinus, who became the personal chaplain to Queen Ethelburh. She married the king of Northumbria, Edwin, so Paulinus travelled with her to the north-east. Despite great efforts, his attempts to evangelise were not successful. In time, the mission was shattered by war. King Cadwallon from Wales and King Penda from Mercia joined forces to invade Northumbria. King Edwin was killed in battle and the queen had to flee south, taking her chaplain, Paulinus, with her.

The royal family fled, and one of its members, Oswald, was sent to Scotland to be educated on the island of Iona, which had won a reputation for being among the best places of education in the land. In 634, Oswald felt the time was right to rid his homeland of the wicked Cadwallon. He met Cadwallon and his army at a place called Heavenfield, and before the battle he put a cross in the soil, making his Christian faith abundantly clear. Against the odds, his small army defeated Cadwallon and Oswald became king.

One of the first things he did was to send to Iona for a missionary. The Iona monastery at first sent Corman, a man of 'austere disposition', who did not go down well with the English. After a while, he returned despondent to Iona, abandoning his mission and complaining that the English were an 'ungovernable people of an obstinate and barbarous temperament'!

The community at Iona held a conference to work out what to do next. Present at this conference was an Irish monk called Aidan, who listened intently to Corman's report. He then rose and said to Corman, 'Brother, it seems to me that you were too severe on your ignorant hearers. You should have followed the practice of the Apostles, and begun by giving them the milk of simpler teaching, and gradually nourished them with the word of God.' When Aidan had finished speaking, the conference fell into silence and all eyes were on him. They sensed that there was a clear call of God on Aidan to go and evangelise the English, and so, without further ado, he was duly consecrated bishop and sent off with the prayers and blessings of the Iona monastery.

Aidan was consecrated in 635 and immediately travelled to Northumbria, meeting King Oswald at Bamburgh on the Northumbrian cost. A few miles north of Bamburgh lies the tidal island of Lindisfarne, and here Aidan formed a mission base of Christian people who were trained in teaching and evangelism. This was one of the most effective mission bases England has ever seen. Here Aidan stayed, overseeing his community, setting up other communities in the north-east and training people like Hilda and Chad and his brothers.

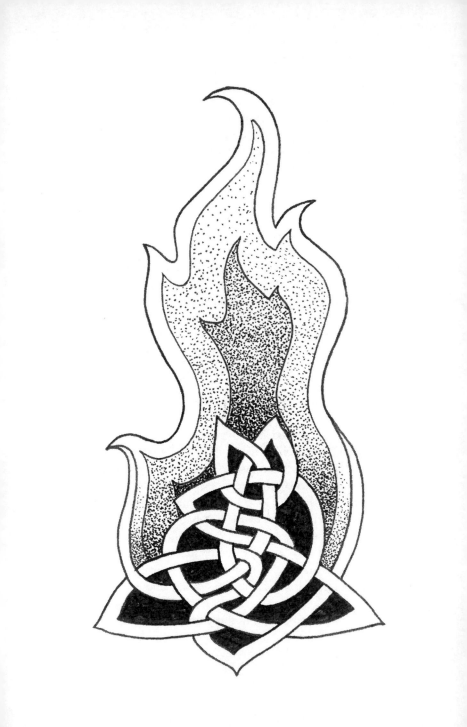

Aidan's ministry in England is significant not so much for what he did but more for the kind of person he was, and for the kind of Christian spirituality and witness he modelled. This was to impress the British people deeply and would affect the Celtic church in England for several generations. The Venerable Bede writes of Aidan:

Among other evidences of holy life, he gave his clergy an inspiring example of self-discipline and continence, and the highest recommendation of his teaching to all was that he and his followers lived as they taught. He never sought or cared for any worldly possessions, and loved to give away to the poor who chanced to meet him whatever he received from kings or wealthy folk. Whether in town or country, he always travelled on foot unless compelled by necessity to ride; and whatever people he met on his walks, whether high or low, he stopped and spoke to them. If they were heathen, he urged them to be baptised; and if they were Christians, he strengthened their faith, and inspired them by word and deed to live a good life and to be generous to others. His life is in marked contrast to the apathy of our own times.[1]

Aidan's example was different from the model of Christianity that was being expressed in the Western European church, which had formed its centre in Rome. By being so closely connected with the former Roman Empire, the church in Rome had uncritically espoused a number of secular values and ways of working. While the Celtic church had its faults, its strength lay in the fact that it had never had much to do with powerful institutions and it formed its life and witness among the poor and the insignificant. Thus there were, in Britain in the seventh century, two fairly contrasting expressions of Christian life.

Both Roman and Celtic forms of Christianity were strongly community-based, and, for both, the monasteries were very effective mission bases. But the styles of monastic life differed considerably. Magnus Magnusson describes these differences, which in many ways summarise the cultural disparities between these two forms of Christian expression:

Celtic monks lived in conspicuous poverty; Roman monks lived well. Celtic monks were unworldly, Roman monks were worldly. Celtic bishops practised humility, Roman bishops paraded pomp. Celtic bishops were ministers of their flocks, Roman bishops were monarchs of their dioceses. Celtic clergymen said, 'Do as I do', and hoped to be followed; Roman clergymen said, 'Do as I say', and expected to be obeyed.[2]

Some would say that this is an exaggeration, but certainly, if we compare the Roman Wilfrid with the Celtic Aidan or Cuthbert, we do see very different approaches.

The eighth-century *Life of Wilfrid* by Eddius Stephanus makes very different reading from Bede's *Life of Cuthbert*. In Bede we hear stories of Cuthbert's austere hermitage on Farne Island and the simple lifestyle of the monks on Lindisfarne. By contrast, Wilfrid, himself originally trained on Lindisfarne, had become attracted to certain values that were uncritically connected with those of the Roman Empire. Thus, where Aidan and Cuthbert were content to build small wooden makeshift dwellings for their monks and nuns, and erect simple churches, Wilfrid was planning far grander things, no doubt sincerely believing that it was in the interests of the gospel and the church to do so. One of Wilfrid's achievements was to build a fine church at Ripon. According to Eddius Stephanus, Wilfrid 'adorned the bridal chamber of the true Bridegroom and Bride with gold and silver and every shade of purple: at Ripon he started and completed from foundation to roofbeam a church built of dressed stone, supported with columns and complete with side aisles'. This was how they were building churches in Europe, and this was seen to be appropriate for Britain. At the dedication of the church, 'Wilfrid stood before the altar, facing the people, and in the kings' presence read out in a clear voice a list of lands which previous monarchs and now themselves had given him for their soul's salvation with the consent and signature of the bishops and all the earldom'.[3] The dressed stone of Ripon was in stark contrast to the Celtic daub and wattle, and Wilfrid's interest in land possession would have been an anathema to the Celtic bishops.

No doubt, both approaches were sincere. The Celtic approach, however, was much more gentle and humble, and therefore altogether more sensitive to the people it was directed towards. Aidan's gentle personality and spirituality were the key to the mission. He had an infectious holiness, which, far from making him remote and other-worldly, enabled him to mix with all kinds of people and to understand their world. They could believe in his message because he was a person whose lifestyle was transparently attractive to all who were seeking God. In Aidan's life, we see the Beatitudes displayed.

The Irish Aidan was, no doubt, deeply influenced by the likes of Brigid. Ian Bradley writes:

For all the legends about their miraculous deeds and supernatural powers they also had a great simplicity and this is one of their most attractive characteristics for us today. When St Brigid, abbess of the great mixed monastery at Kildare, was asked what were the three things most pleasing to God, she replied true faith in the Lord with a pure heart, a simple life with piety, and generosity with charity. These were all qualities that the Celtic saints exhibited very clearly in their own lives.[4]

Concern for the poor

This simple lifestyle meant that the Celtic church had no difficulty in communicating with the poor. Indeed, they regarded concern for the poor as a high priority. Bede tells us of Aidan:

If wealthy people did wrong, he never kept silent out of respect or fear, but corrected them outspokenly. Nor would he offer money to influential people, although he offered them food whenever he entertained them as host. But, if the wealthy ever gave him gifts of money, he either distributed it for the needs of the poor, as I have mentioned, or else he used it to ransom any who had unjustly been sold as slaves. Many of those whom he had ransomed in this way later became his disciples; and when they had been instructed and trained, he ordained them to the priesthood.[5]

It is worth dwelling on the thought that the first theological college in England comprised a large number of freed slaves. Such people were clearly able to understand the poor of the land. It is probably true to say that this was the one time in its history when the English church genuinely lived close to the people. Once it started investing in lands and properties and putting up fine buildings, it inevitably began to grow more distant from the poor.

This church's choice to be poor was probably not an easy one. As we have seen, Aidan, in his closeness to the royal family, would have seen the pleasures that money could buy. We get the occasional insight in Cuthbert's life that he was tempted by wealth. When the young Cuthbert became prior of Melrose, Bede tells us that he would often lament, 'If I could live in a tiny dwelling on a rock in the ocean, surrounded by the swelling waves, cut off from the knowledge and the sight of all, I would still not be free from the cares of this fleeting world, nor from the fear that somehow the love of money might snatch me away.'[6] His longing for solitude led him eventually to Farne Island, but it is interesting to note that he knew himself well enough to realise that simple removal from the world would not mean the absence of longing for worldly things. Perhaps Cuthbert was aware of Wilfrid's growing reputation and wealth. They were both born in the same year, and I sometimes wonder whether Cuthbert, who was by no means entirely critical of all things Roman, did from time to time envy Wilfred's life. If this were so, then Cuthbert becomes even more of an inspiration to those who are seduced by the materialism of our modern-day world.

Aidan's ministry clearly influenced King Oswald and also Oswin, who succeeded him as king in 642. Aidan developed a very special friendship with Oswin, whom he loved dearly. It was a mutual love and one day Oswin expressed his affection by giving Aidan a very fine horse, because he worried about the effect on Aidan's health of the long journeys he regularly made on foot to share the gospel. Not long afterwards, Aidan met a poor man who begged for alms. In response, Aidan gave him the horse. Then Oswin invited Aidan for dinner and, on the way in, took Aidan to task for giving away such a fine horse. If he had known that this was how Aidan was going to treat his gift, he asserted, he would have given him one of his worst horses rather than his best one. Aidan at once answered, 'What are you saying, Your Majesty? Is this child of a mare more valuable to you than this child of God?' With that, they went in to dine. Aidan sat at the table but the king stood by the fire rather restlessly. Suddenly he unbuckled his sword, threw it down, knelt at Aidan's feet and begged his forgiveness. Aidan duly forgave him and Oswin sat down and started to chatter away. But Aidan grew more and more serious until he started to weep openly. All who were present were quite mystified. Then Aidan leaned across to his chaplain, who was near him, and said, 'I know the king will not live very long; for I have never before seen such a humble king. I feel he will soon be taken from us, because this nation is not worthy of such a king.' It was indeed a prophetic word, for only a few days later King Oswin was assassinated.

This was the second king loved by Aidan who had died a violent death. Such were the wounds on Aidan's heart that, only eleven days after Oswin's death, Aidan himself was taken from this world, dying at Bamburgh on 31 August 651. Today, inside St Aidan's Church at Bamburgh, a place is marked that is supposed to be where Aidan began his journey home to Paradise.[7]

Fragile protest movements

The Celtic commitment to a truly authentic lifestyle of holiness, which expressed itself in a way that did not remove the Christians from the people but, through simple living, brought them nearer to them, profoundly challenges the consumerist mentality of our day. The Celtic church would have been appalled by anything to do with the so-called 'prosperity gospel' teaching of the smart-suited tele-evangelists who promise wealth and success. It also challenges the church's use of power and wealth at every level. In the early witness of Christian life in this country, there were two expressions of Christian faith: one that had developed a close association with many of the values and structures of a powerful, though collapsing, world empire, and another that took Jesus' teaching in the Sermon on the Mount at face value and dared to live it.

We can't go back in time or pretend that history has not taken place. We have to start from now, and the fact is that we do have large numbers of church buildings, many of them great and grand and finely adorned. We do have church structures that seem anything but simple. We do have our institutions and committees. It seems to me that the Celtic church would not seek programmes to abolish all of this. Cuthbert was concerned, in fact, to try to bring the two sides of Roman and Celtic together, and to some extent he was successful. What we do need are communities of people who have Aidan's gentleness and toughness: a gentleness to understand the vulnerable and the poor; a toughness to challenge the church when it is seduced by all kinds of power.

When I was writing the first edition of this book, I happened to see a TV version of J.B. Priestley's *A Summer Day's Dream*, with the lead role taken by John Gielgud. This play illustrates well the powerful impact of the message and lifestyle that we see represented in Aidan. In the drama, three visitors find themselves at a large house in the south of England in the mid 1970s. It is imagined that a nuclear holocaust has taken place, and the family who live in the house are some of the few survivors. Through the trauma of nuclear holocaust, this little family has been set free from the conspiracy of materialism, political dogmatism and scientific rationalism that very nearly destroyed their country. When the three visitors arrive, representing those three destructive strands in our society, they are puzzled and angry at the family's 'outdated' lifestyle of simplicity, love for the earth and enjoyment of spiritual values. But the family members do not try to use manipulative methods to control or persuade the visitors. They are simply themselves, and, like those washed up on the island in Shakespeare's *The Tempest*, the three visitors slowly become beguiled by the magic of the place. They are like those who awaken from sleep. By the time they leave the household, something within them has come to life. The small community has become a vulnerable protest movement and is making its mark, albeit with difficulty, on powerful forces.

We need many small and fragile protest movements which are prepared to swim against the tide. It is my impression that the Spirit of God is calling us to consider the Celtic church as a model of authenticity and simplicity, not so much to put the church right but rather so that the church can be freed to live once again, joyfully and confidently, a beatitude lifestyle in our very confused world. In the coming years, many who are wearied by the pressures and demands of this restless world will find themselves washed up on such islands, where they can be reminded of another world— one that, in its simplicity, is full of abundant life.

Bible reading

Matthew 5:1–16: The beatitude lifestyle.

Application

1. If you are involved in leadership at any level, either in church or at work, spend some time comparing your way of leading with Aidan's.
2. What do you feel about the subject of poverty? Reflect on your own lifestyle: are you satisfied with it? Are there things you want to change? Are your attitudes nearer to the spirit of the beatitudes than to the consumerism of our day?
3. To what extent is your church a 'fragile protest movement'? How can your church community become one that helps people to 'wake up'?

Prayer

Lord, Aidan was humble and lowly; forgive us for being proud.
Lord have mercy, *Lord have mercy.*

Lord, Aidan was patient; forgive us for being impatient.
Christ have mercy, *Christ have mercy.*

Lord, Aidan witnessed with constant love; forgive us for being inconsistent.
Lord have mercy, *Lord have mercy.*

O God our mission, whose gentle apostle Aidan befriended everyone he met with Jesus Christ, grant us humble, Spirit-filled zeal, that we may inspire others to learn your ways, and to pass on the torch of faith.[8]

Bible

Boisil

On the night that Aidan died at Bamburgh, a young 16-year-old boy called Cuthbert was looking after a flock of sheep on a hillside overlooking the Northumbrian coast. When the other shepherds had fallen asleep, Cuthbert was in the habit of spending time in prayer. On this particular night, while he was praying he suddenly saw a light streaming from the sky. It must have been a similar experience to that of the shepherds at Bethlehem, because he also heard the songs of the angels praising God. As he looked at the angels, he saw the soul of 'some holy man' being taken up into heaven. He was to learn later that it was the soul of Aidan. So impressed was young Cuthbert by this experience that he decided to join the little Christian community at Melrose, which is near the present-day border of Scotland and England and was then in the kingdom of Bernicia. He went to this community because he had heard of Boisil, who was the prior there and had become well known for his particularly holy life and for his scholarliness. By chance, Boisil was standing by the monastery gate when Cuthbert arrived. Cuthbert dismounted and went into the church to pray. Bede records for us, 'Boisil had an intuition of the high degree of holiness to which the boy he had just been looking at would rise, and said just this single phrase to the monks with whom he was standing: "Behold the servant of the Lord".'

Boisil took no persuading to accept this young lad into the community and we are told that Cuthbert 'watched, prayed, worked and read harder than anyone else'. Cuthbert loved his time at Melrose, and grew close to Boisil. However, as was common in those days, there came a time when the monastery was attacked by the plague, which 'was ravaging the length and breadth of the country'. Both Cuthbert and Boisil were afflicted but, while Cuthbert was healed, Boisil was given the knowledge that he would die and that he had only a week to live. Boisil decided to spend the last week of his life with Cuthbert, studying the Bible. Boisil chose St John's Gospel, and so for seven days the ailing Boisil and the recovered Cuthbert spent time immersed in this much-loved Gospel. Bede tells us that they 'dealt not with the profound arguments but with the simple things of "the faith which worketh by love"'. As they read it, so Boisil received prophetic insight into Cuthbert's life and 'unfolded all Cuthbert's future during that week', even to the extent of telling Cuthbert that he would become a bishop—news that Cuthbert was very reluctant to receive. After a week, Boisil died, no doubt with his mind and heart filled with St John's accounts of the resurrection of Jesus.

The Bible was greatly loved by the Celtic church. The historian Leslie Hardinge writes:

By far the most influential book in the development of the Celtic Church was the Bible. It moulded their theology and guided the worship of the early Christians. It suggested rules of conduct and transformed the ancient laws of Irish and Welsh pagans into Christian statutes. It lay at the foundation of the education of children and youth, and sparked the genius of poets and songwriters. It provided inspiration for the scribes of history and hagiography and affected the language of the common people, becoming the dynamic for the production of the most beautiful hand-written books ever made.[1]

Biblical quotations are found everywhere in Celtic Christian writings. Patrick, one of the earliest Celtic saints, wrote two short works, *Confession* and *Letter to Coroticus*, which have survived to this day. One scholar has counted in these works 340 quotations from 46 different books of the Bible! A paragraph from his *Confession* illustrates just how steeped Patrick was in the scriptures. Here he is defending himself against those who said that he was too unlearned and simple:

But if it had been granted to me as to others, I would not, however, be silent, because of the recompense. And if, perhaps, it appears to some, that I put myself forward in this matter with my ignorance and slower tongue, it is however, written: 'Stammering tongues shall learn quickly to speak peace.' (Isa. 32:4) How much more ought we to aim at this— we who are the 'epistle of Christ'—for salvation even to the end of the earth (Acts 13:47)—and if not eloquent, yet powerful and very strong— written in your hearts 'not with ink,' it is testified... 'but by the Spirit of the living God.' (2 Cor. 3:3) And again the Spirit testifies; 'and rusticity was ordained by the Most High.' (Ecclus. 7:15)[2]

It does not make easy reading for us today, but such passages reveal Patrick's dependence on the Bible. It is interesting to note that, in common with much of the church of his time, he freely quotes from the apocryphal book of Ecclesiasticus.

The pre-Christian Celts were not particularly interested in books. In fact, this has always been a problem for historians: our knowledge of the Celts has often to be gained from non-Celtic books and writings because the Celts preferred to communicate their experiences and knowledge through songs, poems and art. If they wanted to record words, they did so by memorising rather than writing and reading. The emerging Christian communities thus somewhat broke with tradition when they developed their love for the Bible; but then, true to tradition, they learned large parts of it off by heart.

The Bible, theology and vision

The Celtic church developed a love for those books of the Bible that are particularly intuitive, visionary and imaginative. Hence the Celts' love for the Psalms, with their emphasis on creation and their emotional content, for the Celts were a people at ease with creation and with the earthiness of their own emotions. Their favourite Gospel was that of John, who, through his Gospel and his Revelation, showed himself to be a mystic and an adventurer. Traditionally, each evangelist was associated with one of the four beasts referred to in Revelation 4:6–7, who are before the throne of God. Matthew was seen as the beast with the face of a man, Mark was the lion, Luke was the ox (often pictured as a calf), and John was the eagle. The Celts loved all creatures but, as we have already seen, they had a special admiration for the eagle, which was believed to be able to fly higher than any other bird and to see things that were invisible to others. The eagle could 'see and perceive' (Luke 8:10). The Celtic church loved this kind of seeing, and the story told above of Cuthbert and Boisil is typical of the way in which they liked to read their Bibles. They were more than equipped to deal with theological issues related to the gospel but, for the final week of Boisil's life, they read the Bible not simply as a matter of academic study. Instead, they held it alongside their experience of life, and in this instance they were holding the Gospel of John alongside the joint experiences of a dying wise old man and a young man embarking on a new ministry. In their love for the gospel, they dwelt on the 'simple things' (always a complimentary word in Celtic terms) to do with faith and love. And here, in their dwelling on the simple things, they became open to prophetic insight. This story reveals the fact that the Celtic church's approach to scripture was both evangelical and charismatic.

Cuthbert developed such a reputation for his love for the Bible that, not long after his death, Eadfrith, then Bishop of Lindisfarne, began work on an exquisite illuminated copy of the four Gospels in honour of Cuthbert. This book, now 1300 years old, is in the British Library, and it gives us not only one of our finest examples of Celtic Christian art but also a clear indication of the respect with which the Celtic church held the Bible, for the artwork is so evidently a labour of love and affection. It is a spiritual and theological work, and the intricate pictures and borders are there as delicate tools to help us excavate the truths of the Gospels. In fact, the more we study these illuminations, the more we realise that Eadfrith was using them at the same time for theological reflection. If we look closely at his artwork, we notice from time to time some tiny imperfections. There are letters and patterns that are left uncoloured, or a pattern that disturbs the natural symmetry of the page. Dr Mark Stibbe writes:

In achieving such effects, Eadfrith suggested a whole theology through gaps or differences. In pictures which are notable for their order, symmetry and harmony, Eadfrith left deliberate omissions or made momentary departures from the rest of the picture. This remarkably post-modern strategy could be interpreted as Eadfrith's way of deconstructing the sense of structure which he has so elaborately created. In a sense, that is precisely what it is. Eadfrith's motivation for this idiosyncrasy can only have been that he was not prepared to make a perfect picture. Only God is perfect. We are imperfect. To create what appeared to be a perfect portrayal of divine truths would be nothing short of pride and even blasphemy.[3]

The fact that a bishop was giving so much of his time to this work says something in itself about the value the Celtic church placed on the Bible. Leslie Hardinge summarises this:

The Celtic Church cherished a deep love for the Bible, and from the Epistles of St Paul developed their theology. The Psalms were used in worship, and were the inspiration of poets and preachers. Without the influences of the views of church fathers, Celtic theologians set about discovering what the Scriptures meant... unlike the theologians of Roman Christianity who appealed more and more to the teachings of Church and councils, Celtic teachers stressed the Bible. The role of the Scriptures in Celtic Christianity was indeed a vital one, so much so that no thorough study of beliefs and practices of the Christians of Celtic lands is possible without bearing this fact in mind.[4]

This church put its anchor deep into the word of God and was very wary of espousing any pagan customs that conflicted with biblical values.

Our Bibles now, 1300 years on, are printed by the million, with many different versions for us to choose from. We have lost a lot in the mass reproduction but, thank God, most of us are privileged to have easy access to the word of God. In those 1300 years we have seen variations in terms of reading, understanding and interpreting the Bible. We have known dark times, when the Bible was reserved only for the clergy and academics, and light times when it was released to people in their own language. The advent of the printing press and the spiritual surge of the Reformation enabled millions to draw afresh from its life. Great preachers like John Wesley and

George Whitefield demonstrated its power to change lives. Then, in the age of the Enlightenment, the academic world questioned the authority and authenticity of the biblical books, and, for much of the 20th century, the main approach of academics to the Bible was one of suspicion and scepticism. This has polarised Christians, with radical liberals at one end and fundamentalist evangelicals at the other. All this would have mystified the Celtic church, which would have been at neither end of the scale. The Celts would have hated the scepticism of the liberals but they would also have been very uncomfortable with the rigidity of the fundamentalists.

Now that we are moving away from a prevailing Enlightenment culture into a postmodern age, we have an opportunity to reappraise how we approach the Bible. We have much to learn here from the Celtic church, with its humble love for the Bible, its placing of scripture above reason and tradition, its willingness to learn large parts of it by heart, and its determination to live according to its guidance. We also need to recall its openness to the intuitive. In this church we find a healthy balance of word and Spirit, where evangelical and charismatic insights are both valued. The story of Cuthbert and Boisil illustrates this so beautifully—the reading of the word, which leads naturally on to the use of the gift of prophecy. It was the prophetic insight developed during devotion to the word that enabled Boisil to die in peace and Cuthbert to move forward in his ministry with such a secure foundation.

Bible reading

Acts 17:1–12: Paul teaches from the scriptures.

Application

1. How do you feel about the Bible? How can you foster ways of loving it in the way that Boisil and Cuthbert did? What are your favourite books of the Bible? Why do you love these books?
2. Have you ever tried learning parts of the Bible off by heart? Try learning, as a starter, the Beatitudes in Matthew 5:3–10. Once you have learnt them, call them to mind and meditate on them when travelling, walking and so on.
3. Following the example of Boisil and Cuthbert, choose a passage from John's Gospel and become open to the Holy Spirit speaking prophetically to you. It should be said that it is fairly unusual for the Spirit to unfold someone's future in the way that happened to Cuthbert, but the principle is that God speaks personally to his children through his written word. Allow him to speak to you today.

Prayer

A prayer before reading the Bible:

I open myself to the wisdom of the Word of God
I open myself to the guiding of the Word of God
I open myself to the power of the Word of God

Father, you spoke your Word and the earth was birthed
Speak new life to me this day;
Jesus, you came to us as the Word of God
Speak new life to me this day;
Spirit, you awaken me to the Word of God
Speak new life to me this day.

Father, Son, Spirit
Welcome me now to the Word of life.[5]

Children

Cuthbert

As a child, Cuthbert loved to play games with his friends. He was strong and very agile and would often boast of his ability to beat older children at sports such as wrestling, running and jumping. Later, he told a certain Bishop Trumwine about an incident in his childhood that changed his life. It happened when he was about eight years old (AD642).

One day a large crowd of boys were playing games in a field. Cuthbert was among them, thoroughly enjoying himself. Suddenly an infant who was no more than three years old began to reprimand him severely. Cuthbert could not believe his eyes. This little boy stood before Cuthbert in front of the astonished crowd of children and spoke to him as if he were Cuthbert's father. He told Cuthbert that he should not be wasting his time in games, when God was preparing him for something far more important. Cuthbert laughed, along with the other boys, but the little infant then threw himself on the ground and sobbed uncontrollably. Cuthbert began to become concerned and tried to cheer him up, but as he did so the child looked at him and once again told him to give up idle play and prepare himself for the ministry to which God was calling him. The crowd of onlookers were particularly astonished when he referred to Cuthbert as a 'most holy priest and bishop'.

This experience made a great impression on Cuthbert and he clearly carried an expectation that the good things of the kingdom of God were not just for adults but for children as well. He had experienced prophetic gifting in an infant, and he was in no doubt that such gifts were available to the very young.

After Boisil's death, Cuthbert became prior of Melrose. From this community he would often go off on pastoral and evangelistic visits to neighbouring areas. Sometimes, on these journeys, he would take a young boy with him as a companion. On one such occasion, he and his young companion grew tired and hungry. Cuthbert, always keen to use such experiences as opportunities for teaching, asked the lad, 'What are you going to eat today?' The hungry boy replied, 'I was just thinking about that myself,' and his stomach told him clearly that they couldn't fast for much longer without doing themselves an injury. With characteristic directness of speech, Cuthbert encouraged the boy to 'have constant faith and hope in the Lord'. As he said this, he pointed to the sky, showing the boy an eagle flying overhead, and asserted that God was more than able to send food by the eagle. They continued their journey, came to a river, and there was the eagle settling down on the bank. 'There is the servant I was telling you about,' said Cuthbert, looking at the eagle. He sent the boy to go and have a look at what the eagle had brought and, sure enough, there was a delicious fresh fish that the bird had caught. The boy delightedly brought it back, only to be reprimanded by Cuthbert for not giving half to the eagle!

Stories like this illustrate that Cuthbert and other Celtic leaders were always keen to train children in the things of God.[1]

As we have seen, Cuthbert was greatly inspired by Aidan, who also had a love and respect for children. It was Aidan who welcomed four brothers into his community on Lindisfarne. Cedd, Cynebil, Caelin and Chad were Anglo-Saxon boys who lived in Northumbria. It was decided that they should go to school, and the only school in Northumbria at the time was Aidan's community on Lindisfarne. Here, children were trained for mission and ministry.

The school was very small, with only about twelve boys at first, but very influential. At this school, and as part of the family of Aidan's community on Lindisfarne, the boys learned English and Latin. Along with the monks, they would have learnt large parts of the scriptures by heart, and they would have watched the skills of those who lovingly illuminated the Gospel manuscripts. On the island, they would have become involved in the rhythm of prayer and worship, and they would have watched courageous missionaries going off across the sands to evangelise the mainland. No doubt, like Cuthbert's lad, they were taken out on various evangelistic expeditions and learned the life of faith. As a youth, Chad spent some time in Ireland, and we are told by Bede that during this time he and his good friend, Egbert, were 'constantly occupied in prayer, fasting and meditation on the sacred scriptures'. All four boys became priests, and two of them, Cedd and Chad, became bishops.

Children and power

From an early age, children had the expectation of encountering God in supernatural ways. Bede records for us the story of Aesica, who was a two-year-old living in a convent at Barking. As frequently happened in those days, the community was attacked by a virulent outbreak of the plague. Little Aesica became fatally ill and, just before he died, called out, 'Edith, Edith, Edith.' This was the name of one of the nuns, but no one knew why he had called her name, because she lived in a different part of the convent. Sadly they watched him die. A little later, when they went to find Edith, she, unbeknown to them, had also become ill and died only a short while after Aesica. This young infant had been given prophetic insight about one of the sisters as he was dying.

At around this time, there is another story of a young boy who, when dying, received a vision of Peter and Paul coming to visit him.

It is interesting to read such stories, because they are not written with the intention of evoking a kind of 'Ah, how sweet' reaction. The stories speak much more about the Celtic respect for children. Their visionary experiences were not doubted or dismissed as childish fantasy, and their prophetic gifting was welcomed. The thought that God could work only through the learned and the articulate was abhorrent to the Celtic church.

It seems that many of the convents, monasteries and mixed communities must have been filled with the joyful chatter and laughter of children, who were very much part of the community life. Interestingly, the dying child in the story above was offered the 'Viaticum of the Body and Blood of Christ',[2] which is evidence that the Celtic church accepted that children could receive Communion—another sign that they were welcomed fully as part of the worshipping community.

The Celtic church had taken seriously Jesus' teaching about children and the kingdom of God. In the ninth chapter of Luke's Gospel we find a series of events to do with the contrasting values of the kingdom of God and of this world. The chapter includes Jesus' giving of power and authority to the disciples for their mission to the neighbourhood; the puzzlement of the powerful King Herod; the miraculous release of power from Jesus that fed 5000 hungry people; Peter's moment of triumph as he confesses that Jesus is the Messiah; Jesus' teaching about his suffering on the cross; the extraordinary story of the transfiguration on the mountain, followed by the story of impotence as the disciples in the valley are unable to deliver a young boy of an unclean spirit.

By any reckoning, this is a breathtaking series of events, where genuine power and authority are seen again and again displayed through apparent vulnerability and weakness. It seems, however, that it is too much for some of the disciples, because they start to argue among themselves about who is the greatest—that is, who has the greatest power. Jesus' answer is to take a little child and give the child the highest possible value by saying, 'Whoever welcomes this child in my name welcomes me' (v. 48). In Matthew's Gospel we read the words of Jesus, 'Unless you change and become like children, you will never enter the kingdom of heaven. Whoever becomes humble like this child is the greatest in the kingdom of heaven' (18:3–4). Jesus is saying that children should be valued for what they are now, not for what they will be one day.

In this way, the Celtic church would have been very approving of the way children have been increasingly affirmed in the life of the church in recent decades. In charismatic groups, for example, children have been increasingly encouraged to participate more fully in the life and experience of the Holy Spirit. During part of my time working for Anglican Renewal Ministries, Alan Price (then a Church Army Captain, and now an ordained priest) worked as the Children's Officer for the organisation, and it was a great privilege to have him as part of the team. We learned so much from his unswerving conviction that children should be seen as fully part of the life of the church. In the magazine *Anglicans for Renewal*, Alan wrote, 'Children need to be taught not just about the theory but the practice of living in the Spirit. That is where so much of our children's ministry is weak. We teach children the truths of the gospel (the words of Jesus), but do not lead them into doing the deeds of the gospel (the works of Jesus).'[3]

Anyone who has seen Alan working with children cannot but be moved by the way he respects children enough to enable them to become ministers of grace, not only to one another but also to adults. God breathes his Spirit on old and young alike. Churches can pray for healing and they can listen to God for his prophetic word. Clearly children are vulnerable and great care has to be taken to see that they are not manipulated, but we are entering a new era of respect for children. It was this respectful attitude to children that enabled the Celtic church to accept that God could speak through little infants, and that children were a vital part of the church's mission.

Bible reading

Matthew 18:1–5: Children, greatness and the kingdom.

Application

1. Reflect on your own childhood. What kind of awareness of God did you have? How did you pray? How did adults view your faith? If you attended church, what kind of experience was it for you?
2. With these reflections on your own experience in mind, think of children you know now. Do they have faith and, if so, how strong is it? Thinking of Cuthbert's journey with his young friend, you might go for a walk with a child you are close to and make it an adventure of listening to God and discovering things about him and his world.
3. What is it like for children in your church? Do they feel they belong in the life of the church? Many children love action songs and they also enjoy action prayers: can you think of some simple actions to go with prayers you use in home or church?

Prayer

The Father bending down from heaven,
come cradle the child within you
Cradle the child within you.

Jesus, the Son born of Mary whose heart was pierced,
come heal the wounds within you
Heal the wounds within you.

The Spirit poured out for Sabbath play,
come release new life within you
Release new life within you.[4]

⊕

Creativity

Hilda and Caedmon

From its small beginnings on the island of Lindisfarne, the Celtic church in Northumbria grew fast, spreading out in a network of community bases. Many of these centres became large thriving monasteries, and one such monastery was at a place called Streanaeshalch, known more generally as Whitby. This was a mixed community and the first abbess was Hilda, whom Aidan greatly respected and appreciated. Although of royal descent, Hilda had a great love for all people and was committed to seeing a new community form at Whitby in which social distinctions had no meaning.

Into this community came a man called Caedmon, who had 'followed a secular occupation until well advanced in years'. When he came to the community, he knew nothing about songs and poetry. In Celtic communities, when there was a feast, it was a well-established custom that all the guests in turn would be invited to sing and entertain the others. Caedmon gained a reputation for leaving the gathering just as the harp was about to be passed to him.

On one such occasion, he left the party just in time to avoid having to sing and play. That night it was his duty to look after the community animals, and he settled down in the stable to sleep. He then had a powerful dream that changed his life. He dreamed that he saw a man who came and stood beside him and called his name. This man looked hard at him and said, 'Caedmon, sing me a song.' Caedmon was appalled—he knew he could not sing—but this time there was no slipping out of the party. 'I can't sing,' confessed the very worried Caedmon. The man continued to look at him and then calmly said, 'But you shall sing to me.' This visitor asked him to sing about no less a subject than the creation of all things. Suddenly Caedmon found himself singing of the most profound things of God in beautiful melody. We have a record of the opening of this song from Bede:

Praise we the Fashioner now of Heaven's fabric,
The majesty of his might and his mind's wisdom,
Work of the world-warden, worker of all wonders,
How he the Lord of Glory everlasting,
Wrought first for the race of men Heaven as a rooftree,
Then made he Middle Earth to be their mansion.[1]

Bede tells us that this is the general sense of the words, because he is having to translate from the original language. Caedmon awoke in the morning filled with amazement about the dream. He went to see Hilda to tell her about his experience. She invited Caedmon to give an account of his dream before a number of learned people, so that they could assess the quality and origin of the gift. All agreed that this was a gift given by God. Caedmon was immediately welcomed formally into the community, and he was taught about doctrine and history. As he learned about these things, his task was to turn them into poems and songs.

So Caedmon spent the rest of his life in the community, composing songs and poems on all the major stories and events from the Bible, ranging from the first song of creation that he sang in the dream, through to sobering poems on the last judgment and joyful songs about heaven. Just before he died, he had a strong sense that he was in his last days. On the evening of his death, he asked to receive Communion, and then, Bede records, 'his tongue, which had sung so many inspiring verses in praise of his Maker, uttered its last words in his praise as he signed himself with the Cross, and commended his soul into his hands'. Thus died one of the greatest Celtic poets.

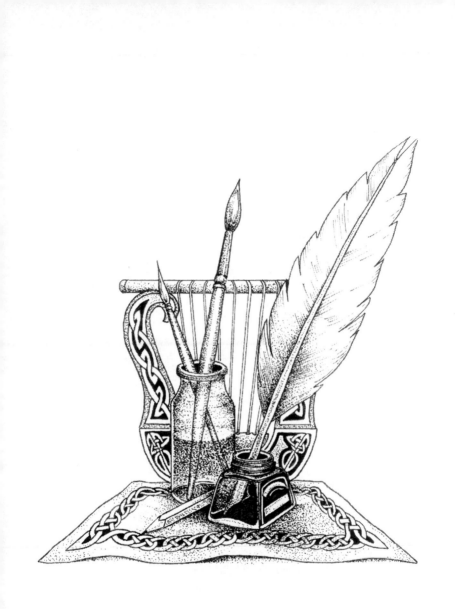

It was not difficult for the Celtic church to accept this kind of creative gifting into their community because, in Celtic society, the bard was a very significant figure. As we have seen, Peter Beresford Ellis identifies for us six basic social classes in Celtic society. The lowest social grading were the 'non-freemen'. The Celts were opposed to slavery, so these people were not so much slaves as lawbreakers. In the next grouping were the people who owned no land and hired themselves out for labour. The third group was made up of those who owned land and worked it. In the fourth grade were the people sometimes described as the 'Celtic nobility', which is a rather misleading title. They were more of a civil service class. The fifth group was the professional class, and in this grouping came the Druids, lawyers, doctors and, most significantly, the bards, poets, storytellers and minstrels. These were a well-trained body of people who were highly regarded in Celtic society. The sixth class was that of the chieftains. Peter Beresford Ellis writes of the fifth group:

The Celts were avid in their pursuit of knowledge, of literacy and learning. This group were the repositories of Celtic folklore, legends, history and poetry. They usually held a salaried position in the retinue of a chieftain. Training a bard was almost as lengthy as training a druid. Diodorus Siculus, Posidonius and Athenaeus have all noted the popularity of music among the Celtic people and mention a wide variety of instruments in use including lyres, drums, pipes, trumpets and a harp-like instrument.[2]

As the Celtic people were converted to Christ, it must have been a great delight to them to find a faith that was so filled with creative life, affirming their inherent delight in music, poetry and art. The Celtic church preferred to communicate in ways that made full use of the God-given gift of imagination. Poetry, storytelling, music and art were all excellent vehicles for teaching profound truths in ways that would not only feed the mind but would enlighten the spirit and warm the heart. It was therefore not at all surprising to find people like Caedmon having a great influence in the community. The only unusual thing in the story of Caedmon is his sudden discovery of these gifts. He became the community bard overnight, whereas in pre-Christian Celtic society he would have required years of training. Such is the disturbance of charismatic gifting!

Gaelic songs and poems

Anyone who visits Cornwall, Wales, Ireland or Scotland and spends time with the people there will soon find themselves in a community with a rich vein of poetry and storytelling running deep through its history. An example of this is a collection of poems and songs (already mentioned in Chapter 2) that were gathered in Scotland many years ago and are still widely read today. In 1832, Alexander Carmichael was born on the island of Lismore, off the coast of Argyll. He grew up hearing family tales of an ancestral connection with the church of Columba, and he fell in love with this Gaelic church and its missionaries. After his education, he found work with Customs and Excise. His duties necessitated making regular journeys to the Highlands and Islands, where the English language was virtually unknown. There, like an excited archaeologist, he started to discover songs, hymns, chants and poems that were centuries old and had been beautifully preserved in the Gaelic culture. He discovered such abundance of this rich resource that he started to make a written collection, largely between 1855 and 1899. The more he travelled to these isles, the more enchanted he became by the prayers, songs and poems. At his own expense he went on many 'collecting pilgrimages', often tramping along peaty paths in high winds and rain to find a remote crofter's cottage where he would stop and collect a further prayer or hymn and meticulously write it down for his collection.

Carmichael's collection eventually reached six volumes, the first being published in 1900. The Gaelic title for the work is *Ortha nan Gaidheal*. The English collection has been given a Latin title, *Carmina Gadelica* ('Gaelic songs'), and is published in one volume.[3] There is in this collection a whole host of hymns and prayers, some of which will sound strange to today's Christian.[4] Noel Dermot O'Donoghue writes of the *Carmina Gadelica*:

The contents of these volumes, hymns and prayers dating for the most part to the sixteenth century, are unique in Christendom in the beauty of language, in the freshness of imagery, and in the depth and immediacy of the piety expressed in a kind of domestic liturgy centred around the homestead and the little world of island crafting communities.[5]

In the collection, we make direct contact with the Celtic love for poetry. It has much to teach our culture, which has given itself so much to prose, inspired by the rationalism of the Enlightenment era. Yet there are clear signs that we are emerging from this particular dark age, and there is no doubt that in the coming years the church will need to rediscover the ministry of the Christian bard. Stewart Henderson, a present-day Christian poet who is acutely aware of the need for the church to recapture its lost poetry, writes:

Thankfully over the past years there has been a realisation within some deep-hearted priests that if you banish poetry and the other expressive arts to the dim cloisters of our faith, then what takes place is in effect the banning of God thinking aloud. But there are still many who view poetry as something of which to be suspicious and to slander as irrelevant. And it is at this point that the English Church, like the country outside its doors, seems to have lost its sight. Not hearing or seeing the full foaming God of the Sea and the Sacraments.[6]

The visual arts

This same suspicion is carried over into the world of art. We live in an increasingly visual age, and yet the church is still bound up in its addiction to words. As a visitor to many churches, I quite often feel overwhelmed by the amount of words I have to receive, whether expressed in the form of a multitude of hymn books, service books and projected words on screens, or delivered from the mouths of the worship leaders and preachers. Thankfully, in recent years and with the arrival of the digital projector, we are seeing more visuals coming into our worship. Art, also, is being taken seriously in some churches as a means of worship. I visited one large church in the USA for their Sunday worship, which was led by the usual group on the stage, but alongside them were four artists at work at their easels, each one interpreting the worship in their own way. There was something very inspiring about seeing each painting emerge as the worship progressed. Also on the stage was a man expressing his worship with flags. Flags have been commonplace in some churches for a while now, but the way he used them was quite different, as he seemed almost to sculpt momentary shapes with the flags as he worked them into the worship. This mix of music, art and dance felt very rich and full of life.

The Celtic church had a deep love for art, and this can clearly be seen in some of the illustrated manuscripts that have survived to this day. A number of these are very well known, in particular the Lindisfarne Gospels, written in Northumbria at the end of the seventh century, the eighth-century Lichfield Gospel of St Chad, and the Book of Kells in Ireland, which probably has origins in the eighth century. Anyone looking at these works will be impressed by the intricate design, the bright colours and the profusion of symbols. Enormous amounts of time and devotion were spent on these paintings. As with Eastern iconography, only those who were considered sufficiently holy were permitted to paint in this way.

Thus the painters of the Lindisfarne Gospels were a team of two bishops, an anchorite and a priest. It is quite sobering to contrast the ministry of the bishops of today's church with that of their counterparts in Celtic times. Today's bishop has to face a mountain of administrative paperwork (little of which is artistically attractive), whereas Bishop Eadfrith of Lindisfarne was spending hours with quills and brushes, slowly copying the Gospels and adding beautiful illuminations. It was a contemplative exercise which no doubt deeply enriched his ministry.

The other expression of early Celtic Christian art that survives today is in the engraved pictures and designs on standing crosses. Many of these crosses are covered with pictures of stories from the Bible. Standing high and proud by roadsides and on hilltops, they served as lively evangelistic tracts for the illiterate, who could come and 'read' for themselves the good news depicted so beautifully in the stone.

Music

When it comes to the music of the early Celtic church, we have fewer resources to go on. Alexander Carmichael tells of the music he encountered in his travels in the Hebrides: 'The music of the hymns had a distinct individuality, in some respects resembling and in many respects differing from the old Gregorian chants of the Church. I greatly regret that I was not able to record this peculiar and beautiful music, probably the music of the old Celtic Church.'[7] According to Ian Bradley, Celtic plainchant had a more 'lyrical, mystical, sinuous quality than the cooler and more controlled Gregorian chant favoured by Rome'.[8] He goes on to point out that Celtic church music was also greatly influenced by the sounds of creation. It was quite customary, for example, for people to stand on the seashore and sing music inspired by the sound of the waves. It is interesting to find, nowadays, a number of recordings appearing in which the music is influenced by sounds of nature—running water, or the cries of creatures like whales or seagulls. Ian Bradley comments on this:

This kind of mouth music, so deeply in tune with the rhythms of nature, is very different from the four-square hymns we have been used to singing in Western churches since the Reformation. But it is perhaps not so different from the Taizé chants, folk-songs and rhythmic choruses from Africa and Asia which are increasingly coming to enliven our worship and broaden our experience of religious music.[9]

It is my conviction that it is a matter of some urgency to rediscover this kind of sung worship if we want what we do in church to make any sense to those beyond it. Our heavy hymns or disposable choruses just do not make sufficient connections with the deep searchings in the lives of so many.

I find it most interesting that Bradley mentions Taizé and African music, for I believe these are two styles of musical worship that we can learn from if we are to connect with the non-church community that has little knowledge of church culture. It is interesting to observe that probably the most effective musical worship in evangelistic terms is that of Taizé, where every summer thousands of non-Christian people flock to the Eglise de la Reconciliation and, settling in the stillness of that vast chapel, encounter spiritual depth through the music, much of which is in a language they do not understand. So much for our desperate need to find words that make sense to a modern generation! The other experience of sung worship that connects well culturally is the music that comes from the traditional communities in the countries within Africa. The group Ladysmith Black Mbazo has popularised black South African music, and many who listen to their songs find themselves being moved, often for reasons they don't fully understand. I am quite unschooled in this music, but something about it tells me that it comes from the heart, and somehow contains within its rich harmonies the range of human emotions.

There is a task before us, therefore, to rediscover Celtic expressions of worship that are in harmony with those who first worshipped the Lord in these lands. Because they were a listening people and profoundly mission-minded, they developed a style of musical worship that worked beautifully. Those who found salvation in Christ through the witness of the church also discovered a way of singing to him that required no abrupt cultural shift.

Alexander Carmichael was clearly greatly stirred by the music of the Gaelic people that arose from their holistic way of life. We would do well today to listen again to Carmichael: 'Perhaps no people had a fuller ritual of song and story, of secular rite and religious ceremony, than the Highlanders. Mirth and music, song and dance, tale and poem, pervaded their lives, as electricity pervades the air.'[10]

Bible reading

Exodus 35:20–35: God inspires Bezalel and Oholiab with artistic gifts.

Application

1. When did you last spend time with a poem? If you have a book of poetry nearby, find one that you like and read it carefully. Note how it communicates to you. Why is it that it speaks to your heart as well as your mind? Perhaps you might write a poem yourself: why not start now?

2. Spend a little time thinking about the Celtic love of art. How much visual communication is there in your church? Can you

think of ways that you could bring more life, visually, to your church building?

3. Think about the style of music that you have in church. How does it relate to people outside the church? Do people have to make a big cultural leap to come into your church? How about going out one day to the sea or a river and starting to praise the Lord in music inspired by his creation?

Prayer

Lord, you are my island, in your bosom I rest.
You are the calm of the sea, in that peace I stay.
You are the deep waves of the shining ocean,
With their eternal sound I sing.
You are the song of the birds, in that tune is my joy.
You are the smooth white strand of the shore,
In You is no gloom.
You are the breaking of the waves on the rock,
Your praise is echoed in the swell.
You are the Lord of my life; in You I live.[11]

⊕

Death and the dead

Drythelm

Drythelm was a devout man who lived in Cunningham, Northumbria. The Venerable Bede tells us of a remarkable event that happened to him in his home. He started to sicken, probably suffering from one of the many plagues that afflicted communities at that time. One evening, his sickness reached a crisis and his family gathered around him, praying for him and willing him to live. However, in the small hours of the night he died, much to the distress of his devoted family. The family remained around his lifeless body, mourning for him. Suddenly at daybreak he sat up, which terrified everyone gathered around the bed, and all except his wife ran out of the room in panic. Trembling with fear, she looked at him, and he turned to her and said, 'Do not be frightened; for I have truly risen from the grasp of death, and I am allowed to live among people again.'

He then related to her and many others his after-death experience: when he died, a handsome man in a shining robe came beside him and led him in what he took to be a north-easterly direction. After a while, they came to a very broad, deep valley which stretched as far as the eye could see. What he saw there was truly horrendous. One side of the valley was bitterly cold, with snow and hail, and the other was intensely hot, with great flames leaping up. Both sides were filled with souls of people who had died, and they spent their time desperately going from side to side in a tormented state. Drythelm took this to be hell, but his angel guide, reading his thoughts, said, 'This is not hell, as you imagine.'

The angel led Drythelm on to a place of dense darkness, which he described as a 'nocturnal and solitary gloom'. Every now and then, this gloom was interrupted by a flame shooting up from a great pit. To Drythelm's horror, the angel suddenly left him. Terrified, Drythelm watched the spurts of flame and, as he looked more intently at them, he saw within them the souls of people being flung in the air, then falling back into the pit. He then heard the sound of 'a most hideous and desperate lamentation, accompanied by harsh laughter'. He looked to where the noise was coming from and saw evil spirits dragging five human souls to the pit. As he watched this scene, a group of the spirits came and started to torment him, though they did not dare to touch him. He desperately looked for help but found none, until his angel guide appeared again, putting to flight the tormenting demons.

They then continued the journey out from the darkness until they came to an enormous wall, the height and length of which stretched as far as the eye could see. Suddenly they found themselves on top of the wall, and on the other side Drythelm saw a scene of great bliss. He saw a meadow filled with sweet fragrance and a quality of light he had never seen in life, and in the meadow he saw the souls of deeply contented people. He then began to wonder whether this was heaven, but again the angel corrected him and said that this was not heaven, and led him on. They came to a place that Drythelm found impossible to describe, but made the former meadow pale by comparison. He longed to enter this place, but the angel would not let him and led him back the way they had come.

On the return journey, the angel explained to Drythelm what they had seen. The place of the terrible valley of heat and cold seems to have been a kind of purgatory for those who came to faith right at the end of their lives. They are apparently helped by the prayers of the living, and their ultimate destination is heaven. The fiery pit is the mouth of hell. The fragrant meadow over the wall is for those who have lived good and faithful lives and are waiting to enter into heaven. According to the angel, those who have lived very saintly lives bypass this stage and go straight to heaven.

Having explained all this, the angel told Drythelm that he must return to his body and live in this world again. And so it was that he found himself back in his bed, terrifying a group of mourners by sitting up alive and well again. Drythelm told quite a number of people about his experience, including King Aldfrid and Ethelwald, who later became Bishop of Lindisfarne, and a monk called Haemgils, who told the story to Bede. After this experience, Drythelm entered the monastery of Melrose and developed a reputation as one who could talk with great conviction about the reality of heaven and hell. Many came to faith as a result of hearing his remarkable testimony.

In recent years, there has been a great deal of interest in near-death or after-death experiences, and much has been written about the subject.[1] When I was a hospital chaplain, I came across two people who had experienced life after death, having been clinically dead for a few minutes in the operating theatre. Both men were quite overwhelmed by the experience, such that they were unable to tell me about it without weeping.

The notion of people being brought back to life is not difficult for Christians because, in the pages of the New Testament, we have the stories of Lazarus, Jairus' daughter, the son of the widow of Nain, and Tabitha, who were all called back to this world after dying. We have no account from them of what they experienced in their hours of death, but it is almost certain that they had interesting stories to tell.

The Celtic church had a much clearer view of this subject than the rather muddled and vague ideas around in today's church. Untimely death was more common because of the ravages of plague and warfare. The arrival of the church, with the good news of the resurrection of Jesus from the dead, was gladly received by the Celtic communities, though they had by no means a pessimistic view of death. In fact, the Druid-led religion of the Celts was one of the first to evolve a doctrine of immortality. They had a two-world view: when someone died, their soul passed from this one to the next, which was a much better version of this world. It was also possible for souls to pass from the other world to this one, so newborn babies would carry the souls of those who had previously been in the other world. The church therefore did not have to convince people of the existence of the afterlife, but it did have to provide clear teaching about salvation in Christ, the once-and-for-all nature of death, and the reality of heaven and hell.

The ministry of the dead

In many ways, the Celts were much more at ease with their understanding of death and the dead than modern-day Protestantism. Despite the imagery of the huge wall in Drythelm's vision, the Celtic church believed that the faithful in heaven were free to pray for the church in this world and, on occasions, to visit with an urgent message, usually in a dream or vision. David Adam writes:

For the Celtic Church it was a very thin line that divides the saints triumphant from us on earth. Those who witnessed before us and are received up into glory are very much alive. They are not men and women of the past, but sons and daughters of God, who are alive now and in the fullness of eternal life. The Communion of Saints is a reality to be experienced.[2]

The Celtic church assumed that those who were particularly good at praying on earth would carry on this ministry in heaven. Thus we have a story of a young boy at the monastery of Bardney Abbey in Lincolnshire, where the bones of King Oswald were buried. As we have seen, Oswald was the much-loved king who was responsible for inviting Aidan to come and convert the English, and it was the custom of the members of that community to go to Oswald's tomb to spend time in prayer. One day, a little boy in the community became seriously ill and no medical help could cure him. So one of the brothers carried him to Oswald's tomb and laid him there. After some time, the fever passed; the boy recovered and was never afflicted again by the disease. Bede, who narrates the story, tells us: 'It need cause no surprise that the prayers of this king, who now reigns with God, should be acceptable to him, since when he was a king on earth he always used to work and pray fervently for the eternal kingdom.'[3]

This understanding of the place of burial as a place where the prayers of the saints in heaven had particular effect was very much part of the earliest Christian tradition. When writing *Requiem Healing* (later published as *Healing Death's Wounds*), I came across a number of catacomb inscriptions that reveal this early practice. The inscription 'Blessed Sozon gave back his soul aged 9 years. May the true Christ receive your spirit in peace, and pray for us' was found on the catacomb of Gordian and Epimachus and dates from some time between AD75 and 200.[4] This little prayer reveals that it was the custom to ask the dead to pray for us. Burial places became special places, sanctified by the presence of the mortal remains of one who had been greatly loved in life, and was still loved in death. Here was a connecting point between life and death, and here was an obvious place not only to remember the one who had died but also to request their prayers for the living. In this way, there was an appropriate Christian interaction between living and dead which had nothing to do with superstition or spiritualism. However, it must be said that this practice did, in time, degenerate into cults of the dead, and in some instances the dead saint became a kind of mini-god and the burial place a worship shrine.

Cuthbert's uncorrupted body

It seems that the Celtic church fairly boldly accepted the practice of the infant church, despite the associated risks of cults of the dead. Though such cults probably did emerge, they never seem to have been a serious threat in the Celtic church. One person who must be mentioned in connection with all this is Cuthbert. As we have already noted, Cuthbert was a man of outstanding Christian commitment, with roots deep in contemplative prayer and the hermit tradition, and with an evangelistic ministry that took the gospel to thousands. He desired to spend his final years on his beloved Farne Island, living the life of a contemplative hermit, but he came under increasing pressure to give up his life of solitude to become a bishop. Eventually, when no less a person than the king beseeched him to become bishop, he was prised off his little island and became Bishop of Lindisfarne. There followed two very remarkable years of pastoral and evangelistic ministry.

It was not long, however, before Cuthbert's body, which had been stretched to its limits, became seriously weakened and he became very ill. He was permitted to return to Farne Island, where he died on 20 March 687, as the brothers around him and those on Lindisfarne were singing Lauds. The body of Cuthbert was lovingly washed and then dressed in his bishop's robes. It was covered in a shroud of waxed cloth and taken to Lindisfarne, where it was buried near the altar in the church. In modern Christian stories, that would be the final chapter, but not so with Cuthbert! For in Bede's *Life of Cuthbert* we are given a number of well-documented stories about healings happening at his tomb. For example, there was a boy troubled by demons who was very distressed and violent. No one knew how to deliver him, not even one of the priests who was particularly gifted in deliverance ministry. Then one of the priests was 'instructed in spirit that Cuthbert could restore him to health'. So he went off to where Cuthbert's body had been washed and gathered up some of the earth where the water had fallen. He put this earth in the boy's mouth, and immediately 'this violent boy with roaring voice and bulging eyes was stilled and fell asleep'. Bede tells us that he awoke from sleep to discover that 'he had been freed from the spirit which had beset him through the prayers and merits of Cuthbert'.[5]

Apart from various accounts like this, there is one final and very extraordinary story about Cuthbert. Eleven years after his death, it was decided to exhume his body so that it could be placed in a new coffin above ground, where it would be more accessible for people to see. On the eleventh anniversary of his death, the original stone coffin was duly brought to the surface and opened. When the monks opened it, they were terrified, for there in the coffin was the entirely uncorrupted body of Cuthbert! The body looked as though it was still alive, with the joints of the limbs still flexible, and the bishop's vestments were clean and 'wonderfully bright'. The frightened monks went off to Farne Island to collect Bishop Eadbehrt, who was on a 40-day Lenten fast. He came immediately and said a most beautiful prayer:

What tongue can talk calmly about the gifts of God? What eye has ever seen the joys of Paradise? That will only be possible when we leave behind our earthly bodies and are received into the arc of Heaven by the Lord Himself. See how He honours the form of an earthly body in token of far greater glories to come! You have caused power to flow from these dear bones of Cuthbert, Lord, filling the Church with the very atmosphere of Paradise. You have bidden decay hold, as you did when you brought forth Jonah into the light of day after three days in the whale's belly. The tribe of Israel, which Pharaoh made to wander forty long years in the desert, you called to be your own people; you preserved Shadrach, Meshach and Abednego in the flames of the fiery furnace and, when earth shall tremble at the last trump, you shall raise us to glory for your Son's sake.[6]

After this, Cuthbert's body was placed in its new coffin, along with a few of his personal belongings. The remains of this coffin, along with his pectoral cross, portable altar and comb, which were buried with him, can now be seen in the Treasury of Durham Cathedral.

Anyone from an evangelical tradition will have great difficulty with these stories of miracles of healings by dead saints and un-corrupted bodies. It all smacks too much of superstition and un-biblical practices of praying for the dead and spiritualism. But before we pass judgment too quickly on the Celtic church, we need yet again to go back to their time in history, long before the Protest-ant/Catholic battles of the 16th century. The Celtic church was thoroughly opposed to any form of spiritualism and, as Eadbehrt's prayer reveals, was concerned to pray only to God, not to the dead.

So what was happening with these miracles 'by the dead' and the uncorrupted body of Cuthbert?

The first thing we must remind ourselves of is the sanctity that the Celts gave to place. As we have already seen, the Celtic peoples had a great love for God's creation and they believed it could be influenced for better or worse by spiritual presences. Because they did not have the separatist view that we have inherited of spirit-versus-matter, they were quite at ease with the notion that place and spirit could influence each other. Ground could be hallowed and, indeed, had to be prayed and fasted over before it could be used for a church or a monastery.

The Celtic church held a view that God liked to use places for special purposes, and these places then became 'hallowed ground'. Places like Lindisfarne still have a certain feel to them, which many of us sense when we go there. And so, when holy people died and their bodies (which, remember, were not despised but honoured as a gift from God) were placed in the earth, that place became somewhere that marked a special work of God. Not only that, but it was a connecting point on earth, to bring together the worlds of heaven and earth. We have a real problem in our own day because we have such a clinical attitude to death, whereby the body is seen as essentially a nasty embarrassment that must be disposed of as hygienically as possible, with the minimum of distress. This does not help the bereavement process, because deep within our souls we need to find appropriate ways of not only honouring the body of the person who has died, but also of establishing a place to come to, which becomes for us a physical meeting point of earth and heaven. A healthy bereavement needs to have a 'sure and certain hope' about eternal life and the freedom of the soul to go to Paradise after death, but we are also human beings who have a need to connect on earth with the things of heaven.

To some extent, the Celtic church was using a Christian under-standing of the dead to Christianise pagan beliefs about the dead. J.A. MacCulloch, in his *The Religion of the Ancient Celts*,[7] devotes two chapters to the dead, in which he makes clear that pre-Christian Celtic society was very much aware of the presence of the dead. They were regularly remembered, had places laid for them with food and drink, and on occasions they needed to be appeased, especially if they had had an untimely or violent death. A great commemoration of the dead was held on Samhain Eve. The Christian church, as it emerged in this culture, took hold of the sharp awareness of the dead and transformed it into something that was quite consistent with the Easter faith it proclaimed. The dead were real but were not frightening. We could remember them, not to appease them but to thank God for them. They were around, not to interfere in our lives but to carry on their life of prayer that began on earth. A new Christian festival of All Saints' Day replaced the pagan festival of Samhain. All these customs were used to reinforce the immovable conviction of the resurrection of Jesus from the dead.

The uncorrupted body was a further potent symbol to the Celtic church of the power of Jesus over death. The prayer of Eadbehrt resounds with this hope. There is no suggestion whatsoever of cultic devotion to Cuthbert here, as Eadbehrt is caught up in a paean of praise to his Redeemer. Here is a true symbol of resurrection life, a kind of parable of Romans 8:11: 'If the Spirit of him who raised Jesus from the dead dwells in you, he who raised Christ from the dead will give life to your mortal bodies also through his Spirit that dwells in you.' There is a sense that the Spirit of God was so active in Cuthbert's body that, for a time, not even the natural forces of earthly corruption could affect it. The body eventually did corrupt, but not for a long time. In 1104 it was taken to Durham, and in 1537 the coffin was opened by Henry VIII's commissioners, both occasions revealing that the body was still uncorrupted. It was not until the investigation in 1827 that only the skeleton was found.

The Celtic Christian community, then, clearly had a very positive view of death and great enthusiasm about heaven. There are many songs and hymns which speak with a longing for that nearer presence of God. They also had a very healthy dread of hell, as the story of Drythelm makes clear. They were acutely aware of the effects of sin and preached salvation in Christ crucified. As we saw in the story of Chad in Chapter 7, Celtic Christians were aware of the anger and judgment of God and would often pray for his mercy. Bede tells us a rather gruesome story of a layman who held a military post in the army of King Coenred in Mercia. He was clearly a carefree person and had been sinful in some way. The king urged him to repent, but he would not. Even as he was dying, he was too proud to repent. Then, just before he died, he had a terrible vision in which he was shown by the devil a book of all his wicked deeds. Thus the man died in anguish of soul, and Bede reports: 'So he is now vainly undergoing everlasting torments because he refused to undergo penance for a short while to win the grace of pardon'.[8] Bede records one or two stories and uses them to warn Christian people not to be presumptuous about their salvation but to remain constantly open to God's grace through regular confession and forgiveness. In these days of easy-come and easy-go Christianity, we would do well to be challenged by these warnings.

In summary, we find in the Celtic church a people who had a very holistic view of death, an appreciation of the communion of saints which was deeply encouraging, a vital hope of heaven, and a sober view of hell.

Bible reading

1 Corinthians 15:12–58: The body will be raised to glory.

Application

1. How do you feel about dying? (Be honest. Many Christians are scared of dying but find it hard to tell others because they feel they *ought* not to fear it.) Allow God to speak to you about this.

2. Think of the Christian people you have loved who have died and are now part of the 'company of witnesses' in heaven. If they are buried near you, perhaps you might like to visit their graves, thanking God for their lives and becoming aware of their prayers for you.
3. How do you imagine heaven? Ask the Holy Spirit to inspire your mind as you contemplate this, and be open to his giving you visions of glory!

Prayer

Christ is risen. He is risen indeed, Alleluia!

Christ is risen from the stagnant ground:
Let all creation rise to greet its returning Splendour.
Christ is risen to tread down the powers of hell:
Let all who know loss and destruction rise to greet their returning Saviour.
Christ is risen to renew the face of the earth:
Let all who are parched rise to greet their returning Spring.
Christ is risen to form a new people of love:
Let all who feel abandoned rise to greet their returning Spouse.

Christ is risen. He is risen indeed, Alleluia![9]

⊕

Healing and miracles

John of Beverley

In AD685, a man known as John of Beverley was made Bishop of Hexham. By any reckoning he was a remarkable person, overflowing with the Holy Spirit in such abundance that miracles featured fairly regularly in his ministry. A key to this was his custom of taking time away from his active ministry to reflect and pray. Bede tells us that 'whenever opportunity offered, and especially during Lent, this man of God used to retire with a few companions to read and pray quietly in an isolated house surrounded by open woodland and a dyke'.[1] This house was about a mile away from the church at Hexham, across the river Tyne. One spring, John came here with his companions for his Lenten retreat. As was his custom, he sent his companions to go and find some person in need whom they would invite to spend Lent with them in their little prayerful community. When the group went out, they came to a village where they found a dumb youth, whom John had already met on his visits there. This poor boy was not only afflicted with dumbness but he also had a serious skin disease, which was so bad on his scalp that he had lost most of his hair. The boy gladly agreed to come and join the community for Lent.

After about a week, John decided it was time to begin helping the lad, so he called him and asked him to stick out his tongue and show it to him. The boy duly obeyed, and John gently held his chin and then made the sign of the cross on his tongue. 'Now say a word. Say "yes",' he said, and the amazed boy found he could say 'yes'. Then, slowly and painstakingly, John went through the alphabet, helping him to pronounce all the letters. He then taught him many words, all of which the boy was delighted to learn. Eventually, the boy was saying full sentences. The floodgates were open and the boy did not stop talking all the rest of the day and all night. Bede remarks that he was like the lame man healed by Peter and John, who could not stop walking and leaping and praising God. In the same way this boy delighted in his newfound healing.

But the lad still had his terrible skin problem. For this, John decided to consult a doctor and 'with the assistance of the bishop's blessing and prayers', the skin healed and new hair started to grow back on his head. By Easter Day, a very happy young man had left the community, with clear skin, a fine head of hair and fluent speech.

This story is an excellent example of the way in which the Celtic church went about the healing ministry. In the story we see a number of important features that were essential to the Celtic church's understanding of healing and the miraculous.

A God of the miraculous

We see that the Celtic church was quite at ease with God intervening miraculously in the affairs of people. There was never any sense of dispensationalism, which says that the gifts of the Spirit were simply for the apostolic age. D.H. Farmer, in the introduction to the revised edition of Bede's *Ecclesiastical History*, writes:

It is unsurprising that Bede's History *contains miracle stories. Not all have the same explanation: some were probably the result of natural forces, psychological factors or apparent coincidence. But all contained some marvellous element* (mirum) *which revealed God's power and care. Some of the stories reveal significant detail of interest to the historian. Although many of them seem to be a stumbling block to the modern reader, their absence would have been an even greater difficulty to Bede's contemporaries.*[2]

There was a very high expectation that holy people would be ready vehicles through whom God could work powerfully. Bede takes care to give authentication of the miracles, and it is often his custom to give the name of the person who witnessed the miracle or who heard the story first-hand, so that the contemporary reader could carry out further investigation. Thus, for example, the story related above was one of several told about John by a man called Berthun, who had been John's deacon but at the time of writing was abbot of the monastery at In-Derawuda. Anyone could have gone to Berthun to have him personally authenticate such stories.

Adomnan, abbot of Iona at the end of the seventh century, was the celebrated author of the biography of Columba. In this, he gave a great deal of attention to the many miracles God performed through Columba. Although the Duke of Argyll, writing in the 19th century, talked about 'the atmosphere of miracles' that pervaded the island of Iona during Columba's time, it is generally reckoned that many of the miracle stories surrounding Columba's ministry are either exaggerated or sheer fabrication. He is even purported to have seen the Loch Ness monster. It was customary among the Celts to commemorate great men by exaggerating their deeds but, even allowing for this, there was clearly a great deal of miraculous activity in those early days of the community at Iona. Ian Finlay's *Columba* is well recognised as a thorough piece of work on Columba's life and ministry, and, while Finlay is dismissive of a fair proportion of the miracles, he concedes that 'Columba must have been a man endowed with immense authority and personal magnetism, and I would certainly accept he had the ability to heal by faith and prayer, and more so since he was among men and women who had never doubted his powers'.[3]

In recent years, it has been the custom in academic circles to 'demythologise' stories that include the miraculous, but, as we leave the Enlightenment era, there is an increasing openness to accepting the miraculous, not least because of the emergence of some very able Pentecostal theologians who are writing from their own experience of it. This was precisely the situation that the Celtic theologians found themselves in: they witnessed God working in marvellous ways, and they reflected theologically on it. Mark Stibbe writes:

Celtic Christians would have been more happy with Westerhoff's circle of theological learning, which comprises experience, reflection and action. For them, an ongoing experience of the supernatural meant that the kind of anti-supernatural bias which we see in most recent theology was unthinkable. Their experience of the Spirit made such rational scepticism an impossibility.[4]

Healing and holiness

Another thing we learn from the story of John of Beverley is that the miraculous is closely linked with holiness and prayer, which meant, therefore, that the delivery of the ministry of healing was confined to those who were particularly holy. This is perhaps one area where their practice would differ from the modern-day ministry of healing in many churches, where teams of lay people are involved in offering healing. During my time with the Acorn Christian Healing Foundation, I visited many churches around the country where teams of people were being trained to offer the ministry of healing during or after Sunday worship. In some cases, these teams were quite large, and the ministry they were offering was extensive, effective and much appreciated. Perhaps the early Celtic church would have learned from today's church in this respect, because, in my reading of their practice of healing, it does seem to have been confined to the leaders. Nonetheless, there are important lessons we can learn from this church, not least that God moved in power through the likes of John and Columba because they were deeply prayerful people. One of the dangers of widening the healing ministry to involve all is that we can easily forget the need to prepare ourselves in prayer and become open to God's power through living holy lives. As we know from Paul, it is possible to do all kinds of miraculous things without love (1 Corinthians 13:1–3), but to do so gains nothing. Miracles themselves have no great value. It is when they are connected to lives that are transparently revealing the love of God that they draw people into the kingdom of God.

There is no doubt that the Celtic church believed that deep intercessory prayer was needed for some healings. Another story of John of Beverley illustrates this. We have in Bede's *History* a first-hand account of a healing of a priest called Heribald, who fell from a horse while he was rather carelessly racing it. After the fall, he was unable to move and lay 'as though dead' with a cracked skull. He was very ill during the night, vomiting blood. Heribald tells us, through Bede:

The bishop was greatly distressed about my accident and possible death, because he was especially fond of me; and he did not remain with his clergy that night as was his custom, but spent all night in vigil and prayer, as I understand, asking God of His mercy to restore me to health. Early next morning he came and said a prayer over me, calling me by name, and waking me out of what seemed to be a healing sleep. 'Do you know who it is who is speaking to you?' he asked. Opening my eyes, I replied: 'I do. You are my beloved bishop.' 'Can you live?' he asked. 'I can do so with the help of your prayers, God willing,' I replied. [5]

We are told that Bishop John then laid hands on his head and prayed for him, then went off again to pray some more. Heribald immediately began to recover, and the next day he was back riding again. There was no doubt in Heribald's mind that he owed his life to the prayers of Bishop John. We also get something of an insight here into the affection that existed between John and his clergy.

Healing and the poor

A third lesson we learn from the story of John and the dumb boy is the clear sense in the Celtic church that the ministry of healing was especially appropriate among the poor. John was concerned to find someone who was poor and outcast with whom to share Lent. When Cuthbert was a bishop and, in keeping with his custom, was visiting the very poor up in the hills, he held a confirmation service. In the middle of the service, some women brought in a young man who had some kind of wasting disease. Bede tells us that the youth was brought to Cuthbert, who 'had recourse to his usual armoury, prayer, gave a blessing and drove away the disease for which the doctors, despite their skill in concocting medicines, had been unable to devise a cure'.[6] The Celtic church could always be found among the poor, and it was here that they delighted to proclaim, by words and works, the loving mercy of God.

Holistic healing

Finally, our opening story illustrates the holistic nature of the Celtic healing ministry. John was as happy with prayer for the miraculous as he was with employing the services of a doctor. There is no sense in this story that the 'spiritual' way is better. It would not have occurred to the Celtic church to make much distinction: they would have recognised the healing of God in the work of the doctor. We are children of the age of scientific rationalism, which loves to dissect everything and work out precisely which bit is supernatural and which bit is natural. There is no way of telling in many of the Celtic healing stories. Perhaps John was simply a good psychiatrist and helped the boy get over a phobia that had prevented him from using his tongue. Perhaps it was supernatural power. Only we, with our modern-day mindset, would want to investigate this question. For the Celtic church, it was not an issue. Through one means or another, it was God who had done the healing, and they rejoiced.

Clearly, however, some miracles were so extraordinary that there could be no 'rational explanation'. There is another very touching story of Cuthbert, who, again on his travels as a bishop, came across a mother who was in great agony. She had already lost one son in the plague, and now her other little boy was dying in her arms. Cuthbert went up to her and kissed the boy, which was a risky thing to do when the plague was so contagious, and then blessed him, saying, 'Have no fear, do not grieve; the child will get better and live.' Sure enough, he did, and there can be little doubt that it was a supernatural healing that saved him. But there is no sense that this kind of miracle was greater than the other. If the church today could regain this holistic approach to healing, we might become much more open to the full range of healing that God longs to give to this world.

Deliverance and nature miracles

Another form of healing that we should mention before leaving the subject is to do with deliverance ministry. The Celtic church had a clear understanding of the presence of angels and demons, and they knew that demons were sometimes responsible for causing personal distress and illness. I don't detect any sense of anxiety about this in the writings about this church, but rather a down-to-earth sense that this was a job that needed to be done, which they took in their stride. As with healing, deliverance ministry was carried out by those who were the most prayerful and holy. Cuthbert in particular seems to have had a very effective deliverance ministry. On one occasion, he was called to bring emergency deliverance to the wife of a sheriff called Hildmer. This woman was a Christian but was 'suddenly possessed of a devil' (which is an interesting point to note for those who debate whether or not Christians can be troubled by demons). Hildmer came to Cuthbert greatly distressed, thinking that his wife was dying, but Cuthbert was confident that she would be released. They rode together back to Hildmer's home and, as they approached the house, the evil spirit in the woman, 'unable to bear the coming of the Holy Spirit with whom Cuthbert was filled, suddenly departed'. The woman was instantly cured.[7] There are no theatricals here: it is all wonderfully straightforward!

Not all miracles were to do with healing. There are stories of Aidan pouring oil on a very rough sea to save some monks whose boat was in difficulty and who were at risk of drowning; the waters calmed after he had poured the oil out. There are also various stories of miraculous events at the mixed community in

Barking. Bede calls them 'proofs of holiness', which is probably a fairly accurate assessment. One is a curious and rather lovely story about the community. There was a time when many men in the community were dying from the plague. The women knew that it was only a matter of time before they too were affected, and the mother of the community started to make plans for their burial. But they could not decide where they wanted to be buried. Then, one night, after they had sung their psalms, they went out as usual to visit the graveyard where the brothers who had died were buried. Here, in the darkness, they sang praises to God, when 'a light from heaven like a great sheet suddenly appeared and shone over them all, so alarming that they even broke off their singing in consternation'. This was a brilliant light, brighter than the midday sun, and after a while it rose up and travelled to the south side of the convent, hovered there for a while and then went back up to heaven. Extraterrestrial-spotters would have been most excited by this! However, the nuns were in no doubt that it was a clear signal from heaven as to where their bodies should lie after their deaths.[8] It tells us so much, this story—about their positive attitude to death, about how they mourned for their brothers, about their openness to the supernatural intervention of God; and it also tells us that God delights to speak to us about the things that concern us, and he may even do it in miraculous ways.

But we should note finally that, although there were many signs of the miraculous activity of God at that time, there was no expectation that all would be healed and delivered miraculously from their difficulties. The mother of the Barking community, Ethelburga, was ill for nine years with an illness that caused her great distress. Bede clearly understands that this illness was being allowed for purgatorial reasons—that her strength might be made perfect in weakness, and 'that any traces of sin that remained among her virtues through ignorance or neglect might be burned away in the fires of prolonged suffering'.[9] There was clearly an understanding that illness could serve some kind of purifying work here on earth. Cuthbert, who was so ill just before Boisil died, carried a nagging pain in his leg from that illness for the rest of his life. There is no suggestion in the Celtic church of pressure being put on people if they were not healed. They were beautifully open to God, walking whichever pathway he chose for them.

Bible reading

Luke 10:1–12: Jesus commissions his disciples for healing.

Application

1. Do you have any difficulty in accepting that God works miraculously in this world? If so, why? Do you have experience of seeing him working in your or someone else's life miraculously? How can you be more open to his working in this way?
2. Think about the holistic approach of the Celtic church to healing. Does this challenge or confirm the way healing ministry is encouraged in your church?
3. Is there someone you could be praying for, who needs healing? Spend some time listening to God to see how he might want to use you in this way. Pray for those you know who are sick, especially for those like Ethelburga who have been sick for a long time, that they would know the strength of God in their weakness.

Prayer

A prayer following Communion:

Heaven is intertwined with earth. Alleluia!
We have taken the divine life into ourselves. Alleluia!
And so now each may say,

I rise up clothed in the strength of Christ.
I shall not be imprisoned, I shall not be harmed;
I shall not be downtrodden, I shall not be left alone;
I shall not be tainted, I shall not be overwhelmed.

I go clothed in Christ's white garments;
I go freed to weave Christ's patterns;
I go loved to serve Christ's weak ones;
I go armed to rout Christ's foes.[10]

The woven cord

In our exploration of the various strands of the Celtic church in the pages of this book, we have done a lot of looking back. And yet, as I write, all the time I feel as if I am looking forward. Looking back at the Celtic church gives me great heart and vision for the future. It is as though God is alerting us to the fact that he has done the impossible before in these lands. He has broken into a society that was culturally confused and riddled with spiritual uncertainty and superstition. He used a group of Christian people who lived a beatitude lifestyle that offered a radical alternative to the decadence of the collapsing Roman Empire. He used a group of Christian people whose faith was so rooted in the Bible that they carried the word of God in their memories, reciting psalms as they walked the muddy pathways. He used dynamic communities of men, women and children, which were simple in lifestyle but rich in spiritual life and love. He used a people whose hearts were gloriously set on heaven, experiencing the remarkable expressions of the power of God, but who were in every respect wonderfully down-to-earth, loving the creation, caring for it and seeing through it the things of God. He used a people who knew how to pray and how to wage spiritual warfare. He used a people whose lives were utterly given to mission, who were delighted to be open to the Wild Goose to take them to unevangelised places with the good news of Jesus, and who loved the people of the land in such a way as to honour their lives and customs, thereby earning their love and respect.

The more I read about the Celtic church, the more I am moved and humbled by it, and the more I am convinced that it is speaking to us today. Not only does the Celtic church speak to our church, but it also speaks about the healing between our nations. In the case of Britain and Ireland, Celtic Christianity has immense potential for healing the wounds between our various nations as we go back to the beginning and discover all that we had in common before the dark forces of human greed and evil caused such damaging wounds, the pain of which still affects how we live today. When I wrote the first edition of this book, we were seeing the first signs of peace in Northern Ireland. Now, as I write, that peace is looking increasingly secure. Those who live there tell me of the conviction that the rediscovery of their common Christian experience prior to the conflicts of English/Irish and Protestant/Catholic carries great potential for healing. There are similar discussions about England and her relationship to Ireland, Scotland and Wales, where in our history there have been many sad examples of political and religious injustice.

But the implications are wider than just for Britain and Ireland. As I have travelled beyond the UK in recent years to the USA, Canada, Scandinavia, France, South Africa and Japan, I have found that this spirituality resonates very deeply with Christians there. It has worldwide significance.

To some extent, there is a feeling that the Roman–Celtic tension is around again today, but this time it is not the Roman imposing itself on the Celtic. It is the Celtic way that is rising up in the hearts and lives of many people to challenge the Roman ways. Simple cells of Christian life are challenging the powerful institutions; charismatic, intuitive giftings of lay people are challenging the tight grip of clerical and ministerial hierarchies; personal commitment to Jesus is challenging cold nominalism; creation-affirming spirituality is challenging the little world of private piety; genuine holiness and authenticity are challenging the artificial glitz of commercial Christianity, and so we could go on.

This is none other than a discovery of a new way of being church. It is not to do with abandoning the old and starting a new Celtic denomination: God forbid! The Celtic way was not to abolish but to change and transform. Rather, our quest is to see the strands of our Christian faith once again woven into a strong cord so that the church at every level might be renewed by the power of the Holy Spirit, in order that it may share Christ boldly and lovingly to a very needy world, to the glory of God the Father.

⊕

Afterword

Liz Culling is an ordained Anglican minister who, after serving in parishes in the north of England, now teaches prayer, spirituality and mission at Wycliffe Hall, Oxford. She has a special interest in spiritual direction. She is the author of *What is Celtic Christianity?* (Grove, 1993).

There have been a number of debates in the last two decades about the importance of a sense of history. The truth of clichés and truisms such as the need to know where we have come from, if we are to know where we are going, have been demonstrated in public life, and TV programmes such as *Who Do You Think You Are?* suggest that this need is just as crucial to our individual sense of identity. Michael Mitton comments in the opening chapter of *Restoring the Woven Cord* that his discovery of the history of the Celtic Christians in these islands felt like a homecoming, and that when he began to share his findings he found a widespread and growing interest in what he was saying. But was this a passing phase?

Almost every year since the early 1990s, I have taught courses on Celtic Christianity or led quiet days using themes drawn from Celtic spirituality, and I find that interest, both here and across the sea in the USA, continues unabated. There is still a lot of ignorance and misinformation about who the Celtic Christians were and what they believed, but, meanwhile, bookshop shelves denoted 'Spirituality' continue to be stacked with new books about the Celts. Some of these will come and go but, among them, titles from the earlier days of the current surge of interest seem to endure.

I am delighted that Michael's book is to be republished, because of the approach he took in writing about the Celts. First, he is interested in the stories of the Celtic saints, and that is primarily how the history of these first Christians in Britain has come down to us.

Second, Michael is not interested in the stories just for their own sake. In picking up yet another book about spirituality, we must ask the 'so what?' question if what we read is to go beyond the point of mere passing interest or self-indulgence. Michael's love for the wider Christian Church and his personal experience of spirituality and mission led him to discern the coming together of a number of crucial strands of the gospel in the surviving evidence of Celtic Christianity. Thus he retells some of the stories of these early saints but does not leave it there. By relating the themes evident in their lives to the Bible and offering practical application and appropriate prayers, he invites readers to reflect on the significance of these themes for their own situation.

Looking again at some of the issues raised, it is clearer than ever that the Christian church could learn so much from reflecting on how the Celts applied their faith in their own context. Some of those issues seem even more pressing now than they did in 1995. Concern for the planet, for instance, has been taken up by the wider world, which often sees the church as part of the problem rather than the solution. The Celts are not examples of proto-green Christians but they do offer insight into what a healthy understanding of the world as the arena of God's glory might look like. Celtic stories of how animals and humans related to each other are not there for us to sentimentalise and thereby distance the Celts from ourselves, but as a challenge to show us what it might mean for the kingdom of God to break into the world in our own time. Similarly, the matter of community is ever more pressing in a society full of isolated and mutually suspicious individuals. The Celts remind us that the gospel is not about my personal self-improvement but about God's design for his people—how we might be a community of the redeemed who offer hospitality and hope for a lost and lonely world. The way the Celts lived out these gospel themes looked different in their time from the way it might look today, but there are lessons to be learnt.

We learn about the way the Celts lived out their faith chiefly from the things remembered about their lives. Above all, they knew the scriptures and learned them by heart. They sought to emulate the lives of the people they encountered in the Bible. They knew that lives soaked in scripture were fundamental to their identity as believers. That is why they stood out and made such an impact upon their world. I believe it is also the reason that other strands of Christian spirituality are to be found among the Celts, such as evangelism, their close relationship with the natural world, prayer, spiritual warfare and the importance of community. These are themes of concern to the internal life of the body of Christ, while other aspects of Celtic spirituality catch our imagination as we work out how to relate to the surrounding culture. The more we fail to ground the church in the scriptures, the less effective we will be in our witness to the world. All these themes are dealt with in *Restoring the Woven Cord*.

Returning to a book that made an impact on us in our first reading can produce very different thoughts and feelings, for we change over time, as do our circumstances. There are some excellent historical and theological monographs about Celtic Christianity that have been produced in the intervening period since this book was first published. *Restoring the Woven Cord* is a different kind of book, however, in that it challenges us to acknowledge the weaknesses of a lopsided faith and apply what we can learn from the past to our own times. There is a wealth of material here for the weaving to continue.

✎

Eric Pike grew up in the Eastern Cape Province of South Africa. He served as an Anglican priest in the diocese of Grahamstown and later as the Bishop of Port Elizabeth. Now retired, he lives in Cape Town and regularly leads retreats and pilgrimages on Celtic Christian spirituality.

I had the privilege of growing up on a Church of Scotland mission station among the Xhosa-speaking people of South Africa. It was inevitable, therefore, that my early Christian experience would be influenced by the spirituality of the Xhosa.

The Xhosa have a great sense of the supernatural and I grew up with a sense of the majesty of God who was both exalted yet very present in his creation. I learned from the Xhosa that God, *uMdali*, was the creator of all and that it was he who caused the lightning and the thunder, who brought the rain and who controlled and governed all. I learned, too, of malevolent spirits who could cause harm and of the closeness to nature in which we were all called to live.

As a teenager, I came to faith in Christ Jesus and came to know the God who, because of my Xhosa background, I somehow knew had always been there. I was later ordained in the Anglican Church in Southern Africa and was blessed to serve in the rich diversity of our country's multi-cultural communities. I worked for a number of years as an evangelist and church planter among the Xhosa people in the Eastern Cape who had been displaced by the then apartheid government.

This was an exciting time of seeing God act in many ways. People who had not previously heard the gospel came to faith, evil spirits were driven out, we saw people healed of a variety of ailments, and the scriptures seemed to come alive in the rural townships as we lived close to nature and as we walked from door to door to share the good news of the gospel. My sadness, however, during this time, was that the style of 'church life' that I was experiencing, though alive with God's life, was somehow foreign to some of our traditional Anglican communities and I felt somewhat on a limb.

Imagine my joy when I discovered books like *Restoring the Woven Cord* by Michael Mitton, *The Celtic Way* by Ian Bradley, *Celtic Light* by Esther de Waal and *Exploring Celtic Spirituality* by Ray Simpson. Here was a Christianity that I was experiencing in far-off South Africa, which, I discovered, was not new but had deep roots in the Christianity of the Celts between the fourth and ninth centuries. I couldn't read enough and felt that what had been so real for those Celts was what I was living and experiencing among the Xhosa people whom I was now serving. This was a great encouragement to me, as it gave me a sense of belonging and an assurance that I was walking along a path which, though it had become overgrown and obscured, was indeed a well-trodden and authentic path.

I was later elected to serve first as a Suffragan, then as a Diocesan Bishop and, in seeking to discover how God wanted me to exercise my episcopal ministry, it was to some of the Celtic bishops that I turned for direction. Martin of Tours became my guide in the simplicity of his lifestyle, his devotion to God, his evangelistic zeal and his love for the poor. Aidan modelled for me not only gentleness and deep strength, but also a splendid example of a bishop who was willing to walk among the people he was called to serve, carrying the flame of the gospel. He showed me how to proclaim and to live the values of the kingdom in a sometimes hostile environment.

Cuthbert was, for me, the model of great spiritual zeal and energy, sensitive and open to the supernatural, confronting the powers of darkness while maintaining a contemplative asceticism. Like Aidan, Cuthbert was prepared to 'resort unto those places and preach in those hamlets lying afar off in steep and craggy hills, which other men dreaded to visit, and which from their poverty as well as uplandish rudeness, teachers shunned to approach' (Bede, *Ecclesiastical History IV*, 27) Of course, I fell far short and continue to fall short of the example set by my episcopal guides, but I rejoice to have splendid Celtic models from whom to learn and who, along with many other Celtic saints, have become my inspiration under God.

Parts of the church in South Africa, led by courageous leaders like Archbishop Desmond Tutu, Beyers Naude and many others, were great pillars of strength and protest during the struggle to bring about the downfall of the apartheid regime. But the church, in our country's new democratic dispensation, now faces different struggles. We are called not only to stand alongside those infected with, and those affected by, the HIV virus, but also to play a role in tackling the giants of poverty, unemployment, poor service delivery and criminality. It seems to me that as God provided his church with the resources to withstand the heresy of apartheid, our prayer ought now to be that he will raise up leaders who will lead the people of God to express the same fervour and zeal as our Celtic 'models', so that we can in our day build an adventurous and courageous church. A church rooted in small and mid-sized communities, living and proclaiming the values of the kingdom. A church that will be present on the streets and in the homes of our people. A church that takes seriously the ecological crisis facing our nation and looks to our transcendent, yet immanent God as revealed in Jesus our Lord and in the scriptures. A church that loves its Lord and serves in the power of the Spirit. Though the challenges we face are different from those faced by the Celtic church, I do believe that, as we look to our Celtic guides of the fourth to the ninth centuries, we will find the inspiration to guide and lead us in facing the challenges of our nation today.

Ray Simpson is the international guardian of The Community of Aidan and Hilda and its principal liturgist. He is the author of many books on Celtic spirituality and the emerging church. He lives on the Holy Island of Lindisfarne near to the Community's retreat house and study centre.

Michael Mitton dedicated the first edition of this book to his six co-founders in The Community of Aidan and Hilda, whose Way of Life calls us to weave together the God-given strands of Christianity that have become separated. Over the ensuing 15 years, I have been privileged, as the Community's International Guardian, to receive reports from those who follow this Way of Life on four continents of how they attend to their weaving.

Weaving is an everyday thing but it does not come naturally to everyone: it is an art that has to be learned. It should not be disdained as something that diminishes what is distinctive, or reduced to a Facebook thread. Rather, by complement and contrast, it brings out the essential purpose of each strand and the glory of the whole. Here are some examples.

A Quaker commits to seek God in the 'deep silence', but also attends mass once a month. A Pentecostal, becoming awed by the sacred nature of sacrament, joins a church network within the Apostolic Succession. A social crusader who once regarded worship as an expendable luxury now jealously guards the balance of prayer and action. Baptists use Orthodox liturgy and pray with icons. A man who practises deep meditation also co-founds a charity to save the Brazilian rainforest. Protestants learn Ignatian ways of praying. An Orthodox uses contemporary as well as ancient Eastern liturgy. Staff at our Open Gate Retreat House, on Holy Island, lead retreats based on 'The Two Books'—Scripture and Nature.

Some followers of our Way of Life come from strands not envisaged 15 years ago, and find a creative challenge in the invitation to weave. For example, there is the pagan who readily embraces Jesus but finds it harder to embrace church, or the progressive who embraces equality but finds it upsetting to embrace scripture. For others, the cloth they weave has broadened to encompass strands from other faiths that are true, mindful, pure or lovely (Philippians 4:8).

Strands of indigenous spirituality and sacred place wait to be woven into broader cloth. I am glad that Matt Lamont has published *Australian Prayer Rhythms*, drawing on Aboriginal spirituality. An English man had a vision of a reservoir sustained only by a pipe that filled it with water from elsewhere. The pipe and the reservoir began to dry up. Then, disused wellsprings were rediscovered and restored. They represent the life-giving Welsh heritage. In the Celtic tradition, it is possible for a person to go into exile from their homeland and, in giving their lives to a new people, to reconnect those people with their own lost treasures. In our global village, the distinctive strand of a Cornwall, a Wales, or a First Nation people is being rediscovered. Thus the poet Kenneth Steven has Columba coming to a new place:

Here at the water meadow's end he finds the Christ ripe in his heart,
His lips brim with words that soar like larks in the sky,
Almost as if some spring of light and joy wells from the ground beneath.

I myself have been stirred by Thomas Merton's vision:

If I can unite in myself the thought and devotion of Eastern and Western Christendom, the Greek and Latin Fathers, the Russian with the Spanish mystics, I can prepare in myself the reunion of divided Christians. From that secret and unspoken unity in myself can eventually come a visible and manifest unity of all Christians.[1]

This is a call to weave together different spiritualities in ourselves, in an organic way. How may we do this? I have learnt from people such as Chiara Lubich of the *Focolare* movement to make an act of unity with Jesus in various focal places. I make an act of unity with Jesus in scripture (the Evangelical strand) and in Holy Communion (the Sacramental strand); in the poor (the Justice strand) and in the deep heart's core (the Mystical strand); in the spiritual shepherds (the Catholic strand) and in the Living Tradition (the Orthodox strand); in nature (the Creation strand) and in the group process (the Community strand). These acts of unity do not require me to be unfaithful to anything I have learnt of Jesus.

Certain strands that once were barely noticed are now coming into prominence, such as soul friendship, pilgrimage and the bardic singing that often accompanies revivals. There is yet another strand, one that has a hidden strength. The Celtic Christians of whom Michael writes were shaped by the ascetic lives of the Desert Fathers and Mothers. This desert thread of deep roots and daily disciplines is now being recovered by Christians of varied backgrounds and is sometimes termed 'a new monasticism'. Our members in Norway, which threw out monasteries at the Reformation, visit Coptic monasteries. The Coptic Bishop, Thomas, advises them and leads them in wilderness retreats. Inspired by this, Sven Aarsmundveit has published in Norwegian a training manual entitled *Athletes of Christ*. This, I think, is the way the Spirit is now blowing us. We are called to weave together not only threads of bright colour that catch our attention, but also those of deeper hues, whose quality never fades.

❧

Jack Stapleton is an Episcopal priest in Colorado. He served as Guardian of the Order of St Aidan (Community of Aidan and Hilda in the USA) from 1994 to 2009 and as editor of its publication *The Wild Goose*.

'To many, perhaps to most people outside the small company of the great scholars, past and present, "Celtic" of any sort is, nonetheless, a magic bag, into which anything may be put, and out of which almost anything may come.' This comment by J.R.R. Tolkien seems an odd way to begin a reflection on Celtic Christianity as a source of renewal and inspiration. However, Tolkien's warning, given in the context of a scholarly address in his field of philology, is relevant to Celtic Christianity as well. Celtic Christianity developed out of a culture radically different from ours, which formed an understanding of the world of the spirit, the nature of creation, the character of relationship and the value of personal sacrifice. The Celtic peoples of the western edge of Europe were relatively untouched by the urban and centralised culture of the Roman Empire. The culture of the Celtic tribes gave a flavour to the life of Christian discipleship, distinct from that which flowered on the continent. Looking back at the writings of the Celtic saints through the lens of our urban, technological and fragmented world, the aspect of Celtic Christian spirituality that stands out most starkly to me is wholeness.

That wholeness is what first drew me to this spirituality. That wholeness came from a society generally free of the dichotomy of spirit and matter, sacred and secular, that characterises much of Western thought. Such wholeness does not characterise the world in which I live, much less the religious life I've experienced, yet what it first communicated to me was hope. My life in Christ has been shaped by many of the fragmented spiritualities of our times:

evangelical, charismatic, catholic, liberal. I was torn between my natural inclination towards the active life and a yearning towards the depth of the contemplative life. The testimony of the Celtic Christians taught me first of all that I did not have to choose between these various streams.

Since 1994, I've been following an intentional Way of Life from the Community of Aidan and Hilda. It's not simply an updated version of the extant Rules of the Celtic communities. Rather, it is inspired by the record of their lives. In one sense, calling this a 'Celtic Christian' way is unnecessary, but, once you move beyond the adjective 'Celtic', the pattern of wholeness is wonderfully attractive in itself. One acquaintance remarked that there was nothing in this way that she hadn't seen in other groups or traditions. What she had not seen before was all of the elements together.

Following this pattern has not been easy. The spirit/matter, sacred/secular, active/contemplative dichotomies are deeply ingrained in our world—and in me. Even with a Way of Life and a community that shares that Way, it's very much like swimming against the flow of a river in spring flood. What keeps me from discouragement is what makes the adjective 'Celtic' relevant still. The Celtic saints provide me with models of what this way is supposed to look like.

The structure of Michael's book allows me to see those early models more clearly. The stories are very human stories that I can share with my congregation and with my companions in community. They have helped shape a way of life that is slowly transforming a very traditional, institutional church. Though fascination with things Celtic may wax and wane in popular imagination, the hunger for wholeness is both sharp and steady. I rejoice that *Restoring the Woven Cord* is coming back in print and fervently hope it will be available to us again in the US.

Notes

Preface to Second Edition

1 Philip Sheldrake, *Living Between Worlds* (DLT, 1995), p. 2.
2 Ian Bradley, *Celtic Christianity* (Edinburgh University Press, 1999), p. 189.

Chapter 2: Prayer

1 From *The Confession of Patrick*, trans. C.H.H. Wright, in Noel Dermot O'Donoghue, *Aristocracy of Soul* (DLT, 1987), p. 105.
2 Martin Palmer, *Living Christianity* (Element, 1993), p. 69.
3 Bede, *Ecclesiastical History of the English People* (Penguin, 1955; revised edn 1990), p. 150.
4 Bede, *The Life of Cuthbert*, in *The Age of Bede* (Penguin, 1965; revised edn 1988), p. 57.
5 David Adam, *Power Lines* (Triangle, 1992).

Chapter 3: Spiritual battle

1 Noel Dermot O'Donoghue, *The Mountain Behind the Mountain* (T&T Clark, 1993), p. 23.
2 Graham Dow, *Those Tiresome Intruders* (Grove Pastoral No. 41), p. 4.
3 Bede, *Life of Cuthbert*, in *Age of Bede*, p. 59.
4 Bede, *Life of Cuthbert*, in *Age of Bede*, p. 66.
5 Bede, *Ecclesiastical History*, p. 181.
6 Russ Parker, *Healing Wounded History* (DLT, 2001), p. 15.
7 Parker, *Healing Wounded History*, pp. 37–38. His reference to Peter Berg is quoted in Howard Clinebell, *Ecotherapy* (Howarth Press, 1996), p. 56.

8   *Confession of Patrick*, 20, in O'Donoghue, *Aristocracy*, p. 106.

9   Better known is C.F. Alexander's translation, 'I bind unto myself today the strong name of the Trinity'. Both versions are given in David Adam, *The Cry of the Deer* (Triangle, 1987). His book is based on Patrick's prayer, which was sometimes called 'The cry of the deer' following the legend that, after Tara, Patrick turned into a deer and ran free.

10 David Adam, *Tides and Seasons* (Triangle, 1989), p. 105.

11 From *A Morning Office in Celtic Tradition suitable for Michaelmas and Thursdays* (Community of Aidan and Hilda).

Chapter 4: Ministry of women

1   Peter Beresford Ellis, *Celtic Inheritance* (Constable, 1992), p. 20.

2   Nora Chadwick, *The Celts* (Penguin, 1971).

3   Shirley Toulson, *The Celtic Year* (Element, 1993), p. 80.

4   Mary Calvert, *God to Enfold Me* (Grail, 1993).

5   Christopher Bamford and William Parker Marsh, *Celtic Christianity, Ecology and Holiness* (Floris Books, 1986).

6   Bede, *Ecclesiastical History*, pp. 245ff.

7   Bede, *Ecclesiastical History*, p. 244.

8   For a novel on the life of Hilda, read *Hilda* by Anne Warin Marshall (Morgan and Scott, 1989).

9   O'Donoghue, *Aristocracy*, p. 73.

10 Quoted in Esther de Waal, *The Celtic Vision* (DLT, 1988), p. 198. It is a shortened form of the original, which can be found in *Carmina Gadelica* 111, pp. 161–163.

11 From *A St Brigid Night Office* (Community of Aidan and Hilda).

Chapter 5: Wild Goose

1   The story of Brendan's voyage can be found in *The Age of Bede*. The iceberg story is on pp. 236–237.

2   O'Donoghue, *Aristocracy*, p. 43.

3   *Confession of Patrick*, 25, in O'Donoghue, *Aristocracy*, p. 108.
4   Bede, *Life of Cuthbert*, in *Age of Bede*, p. 83.
5   Elizabeth Culling, *What is Celtic Christianity?* (Grove Spirituality No. 45, 1993).
6   Quoted in Robert Van de Weyer, *Celtic Fire* (DLT, 1990), p. 30.
7   David Adam, *The Open Gate* (Triangle, 1994), p. 1.
8   Toulson, *Celtic Year*, p. 120.
9   From *An Office for St Brendan's Day* (Community of Aidan and Hilda).

Chapter 6: Community

1   Beresford Ellis, *Celtic Inheritance*, p. 16.
2   de Waal, *Celtic Vision*, p. 12.
3   Ian Bradley, *The Celtic Way* (DLT, 1993), p. 70.
4   Ray Simpson, *A Pattern of Worship for St David's Day* (Community of Aidan and Hilda, 1994).
5   There are a number of books on the subject of soul friends and spiritual direction. Many people have found Kenneth Leech's *Soul Friend* (DLT, new edn 1994) very helpful.
6   From *A Morning Office in the Celtic Tradition for Trinity Season and Mondays* (Community of Aidan and Hilda).

Chapter 7: Creation

1   Quoted in Van de Weyer, *Celtic Fire*, pp. 33–34.
2   Ian Finlay, *Columba* (Gollancz, 1979), p. 107.
3   Calvin Miller, *The Path of Celtic Prayer* (BRF, 2008).
4   Miller, *Path of Celtic Prayer*, p.86
5   David Adam, *Borderlands* (SPCK, 1991), p. viii.
6   O'Donoghue, *Mountain Behind the Mountain*, p. 30.
7   David Adam, *Eye of the Eagle* (Triangle, 1990), p. 11.
8   See *Age of Bede*, pp. 68, 69.
9   See Bede, *Ecclesiastical History*, pp. 209–210.

10 Euros Bowen, *Gwreiddyn Tap (Tap Root)* (Church in Wales Publications, 1993), pp. 132–133.
11 From *Midday Office* (Community of Aidan and Hilda).

Chapter 8: Evangelism

1   Bede, *Life of Cuthbert*, Chapter 9 in *Age of Bede*.
2   Bradley, *Celtic Way*, pp. 74ff.
3   Van de Weyer, *Celtic Fire*, p. 4.
4   Bede, *Ecclesiastical History*, p. 197.
5   Bede, *Ecclesiastical History*, p. 180.
6   The 'Healing on the Streets' movement is currently growing and developing. Information is probably best obtained by searching the web.
7   Bede, *Ecclesiastical History*, p. 150.
8   Used in *The Vigil of Fire* (Community of Aidan and Hilda).

Chapter 9: Prophecy

1   Richard Harries, *Art and the Beauty of God* (Mowbray, 1993), p. 87.
2   Dan Dychman, *Hidden Dimensions* (Limited Editions, 1994), p. 5.
3   Bede, *Life of Cuthbert*, in *Age of Bede*, p. 57.
4   The stories of Aelfflaed, Ecgfrith and Cuthbert can be found in Bede's *Life of Cuthbert*, Chapters 23—27.
5   O'Donoghue, *Aristocracy*, p. 11.
6   The story can be found in Bede, *Ecclesiastical History*, pp. 104ff.
7   From *A Pattern of Worship for St Fursey's Day* (Community of Aidan and Hilda).

Chapter 10: Authenticity

1   Bede, *Ecclesiastical History*, p. 150.
2   Magnus Magnusson, *Lindisfarne, the Cradle of Island* (Oriel Press, 1984), p. 58.
3   Eddius Stephanus, *Life of Wilfrid*, Chapter 17 in *Age of Bede*, p. 123.
4   Bradley, *Celtic Way*, p. 14.
5   Bede, *Ecclesiastical History*, p. 54.
6   Bede, *Life of Cuthbert*, in *Age of Bede*, p. 54.
7   The story is related in Bede, *Ecclesiastical History*, Chapter 14.
8   From *An Office for St Aidan's Day* (Community of Aidan and Hilda).

Chapter 11: Bible

1   L. Hardinge, *The Celtic Church in Britain* (SPCK, 1972), p. 29.
2   *Confession of Patrick*, 11, in O'Donoghue, *Aristocracy*, p. 103.
3   Mark Stibbe, 'The Revival of Anglican Theology: Lessons from Celtic Christianity' in *Anglicans for Renewal*, Vol. 56 (Spring 1994). Details of this magazine from Anglican Renewal Ministries, 42 Friar Gate, Derby DE1 1DA.
4   Hardinge, *Celtic Church in Britain*, p. 51.
5   General prayers (Community of Aidan and Hilda).

Chapter 12: Children

1   The story can be found in Bede, *Life of Cuthbert*, in *Age of Bede*, Chapter 12.
2   The word *viaticum* literally means 'provision for a journey'. Traditionally it was the giving of the Communion to one who was dying.
3   In an article entitled 'Children of the Kingdom' in *Anglicans for Renewal*, Vol. 55, p. 7.
4   General prayers (Community of Aidan and Hilda).

Chapter 13: Creativity

1   Bede, *Ecclesiastical History*, pp. 248–249.
2   Beresford Ellis, *Celtic Inheritance*, p. 19.
3   Alexander Carmichael, *Carmina Gadelica* (Floris Books, 1992).
4   Some people reading the *Carmina Gadelica* will struggle with such terms as 'incantations' and 'charms', and will be fairly suspicious about talk of fairies! In my view, some of the poems and chants do seem to be fairly superstitious and a few appear occult. But it is absolutely essential that we don't apply rationalistic evangelical presuppositions to our study of these writings. Few of us who live in English suburbia have any idea how the hearts and minds of the inhabitants of the Western Isles work, and we will need to approach these writings with a humble sense of exploration rather than with a censor's pen.
5   O'Donoghue, *Mountain Behind the Mountain*, p. 41.
6   Stewart Henderson, 'If Albion Could Sing Again' in *Anglicans for Renewal*, Vol. 58, p. 12.
7   Carmichael, in his introduction to *Carmina Gadelica*, p. 29.
8   Bradley, *Celtic Way*, p. 91.
9   Bradley, *Celtic Way*, p. 92.
10 Carmichael, *Carmina Gadelica*, p. 29.
11 Echoes a prayer attributed to Columba, in Calvert, *God to Enfold Me*, pp. 121–122. It is used by The Community of Aidan and Hilda in the evening office.

Chapter 14: Death and the dead

1   See Dr Maurice Rawling, *Beyond Death's Door* (Nelson, 1978) and *Before Death Comes* (Sheldon Press, 1980) and Raymond Moody, *Life after Life* (Bantam, 1983). These are full of accounts of those who have returned from death experiences. Paul and Linda Badham, *Immortality or Extinction* (SPCK, 1984) is a much

more scholarly work on the subject. See also *Healing Death's Wounds* (Eagle, 2002) by Russ Parker and myself.
2   Adam, *Cry of the Deer*, p. 75.
3   Bede, *Ecclesiastical History*, p. 162.
4   Mitton and Parker, *Healing Death's Wounds*, p. 52.
5   Bede, *Life of Cuthbert*, in *Age of Bede*, p. 95.
6   *Age of Bede*, p. 97.
7   J.A. MacCulloch, *The Religion of the Ancient Celts* (Constable, 1911; paperback edn 1992), Chapters 10 and 22.
8   Bede, *Ecclesiastical History*, pp. 290ff.
9   Morning Prayer in *Celtic Tradition for Sundays and Eastertide* (Community of Aidan and Hilda).

Chapter 15: Healing and miracles

1   Bede, *Ecclesiastical History*, p. 267.
2   Bede, *Ecclesiastical History*, pp. 26ff.
3   Finlay, *Columba*, p. 173.
4   Stibbe, 'Revival of Anglican Theology', in *Anglicans for Renewal*, Vol. 56.
5   Bede, *Ecclesiastical History*, p. 274.
6   Bede, *Life of Cuthbert*, in *Age of Bede*, p. 83.
7   *Age of Bede*, pp. 61ff.
8   Bede, *Ecclesiastical History*, pp. 217ff.
9   Bede, *Ecclesiastical History*, p. 219.
10   *A Eucharist in the Celtic Tradition* (Community of Aidan and Hilda).

Afterword

1   Thomas Merton, *Conjectures of a Guilty Bystander* (Doubleday, 1966), p. 21.